AF530660

THE GREAT PLATFORM AT VIJAYANAGARA

VIJAYANAGARA RESEARCH PROJECT MONOGRAPH SERIES

General Editors
JOHN M. FRITZ, University of Pennsylvania
GEORGE MICHELL, London
R. GOPAL, Karnataka Department of Archaeology and Museums

Vol. 1 *Pots and Palaces* by Carla M. Sinopoli

Vol. 2 *The Ramachandra Temple at Vijayanagara* by Anna L. Dallapiccola, John M. Fritz, George Michell and S. Rajasekhara

Vol. 3 *The Vijayanagara Courtly Style* by George Michell

Vol. 4 *Religious Traditions at Vijayanagara as Revealed through its Monuments* by Anila Verghese

Vol. 5 *The Irrigation and Water Supply Systems of Vijayanagara* by Dominic J. Davison-Jenkins

Vol. 6 *Sculpture at Vijayanagara: Iconography and Style* by Anna L. Dallapiccola and Anila Verghese

Vol. 7 *Anegondi: Architectural Ethnography of a Royal Village* by Natalie Tobert

Vol. 8 *Vijayanagara: Architectural Inventory of the Sacred Centre* (in 3 volumes) by George Michell and Phillip B. Wagoner

Vol. 9 *King, Court and Capital: An Anthology of Kannada Literary Sources from the Vijayanagara Period* translated by C.T.M. Kotraiah and edited by Anna L. Dallapiccola

Vol. 10 *Vijayanagara: Archaeological Exploration, 1990-2000, Papers in Memory of Channabasappa S. Patil* (in 2 parts) by John M. Fritz, Robert P. Brubaker and Teresa P. Raczek, with the assistance of George Michell

Vol. 11 *Daroji Valley: Landscape History, Place, and the Making of a Dryland Reservoir System* by Kathleen D. Morrison

Vol. 12 *The Great Platform at Vijayanagara: Architecture & Sculpture* by Anna L. Dallapicola

Jacket Illustration:
Central Asian Dancers
Great Platform, Phase I, South Face
Drawing by Graham Reed

THE GREAT PLATFORM AT VIJAYANAGARA

Architecture & Sculpture

Anna L. Dallapiccola
with a chapter on Architectural Features by George Michell

MANOHAR
AMERICAN INSTITUTE OF INDIAN STUDIES
2010

First published 2010

© Anna L. Dallapiccola and George Michell, 2010

All rights reserved. No part of this publication may be reproduced or transmitted, in any form or by any means, without the prior permission of the author and the publisher

ISBN 978-81-7304-858-6

Published by
Ajay Kumar Jain *for*
Manohar Publishers & Distributors
4753/23 Ansari Road, Daryaganj
New Delhi 110 002

Printed at
Salasar Imaging Systems
Delhi 110 035

CONTENTS

PREFACE AND ACKNOWLEDGEMENTS

This, the twelfth volume in our Vijayanagara Research Project Monograph Series, is dedicated to the Great Platform in the Royal Centre, known to most visitors to Hampi today as the Mahanavami Dibba. Our investigation of this monument dates back no less than 15 years, when Anna L. Dallapiccola began a fastidious catalogue of the innumerable carvings with which the four sides of this monument are embellished. Her comprehensive descriptions of the friezes, the first ever to be compiled, form the core of the present volume. John M. Fritz has also been involved in this project, and his archaeological study of the Great Platform roughly coincided with the most recent clearing work of the monument on the part of the Archaeological Survey of India. But since the Survey's findings have yet to be published and Fritz has yet to complete his analysis we have decided to proceed to publication without his contribution, which we hope to issue separately. George Michell has also been involved in this project, and in this volume has authored the chapter on the architectural features of the monument.

As will be clear from Dallapiccola's introduction, the identification of the Great Platform with the spectacular Mahanavami festival that was celebrated annually at Vijayanagara has always been assumed by scholars in the past, but should not be accepted as an established historical fact. Her analysis of the carvings, in fact, would suggest quite otherwise. As Dallapiccola points out in her opening chapter, none of the royal topics illustrated in the art of the Great Platform can be related to the Mahanavami. (This is in striking contrast to the friezes covering the compound walls of the nearby Ramachandra temple that appear to be depictions of the Mahanavami parades.) If any festival is illustrated on the Great Platform it is probably the Vasantotsava, which is associated with the spring season. Dallapiccola's scrutiny of the accounts of the Mahanavami on the part of the foreign visitors to Vijayanagara sheds further doubts on the link between the monument and the Mahanavami. Indeed, the processions of animals, troops and courtly women in the presence of the Vijayanagara king, as reported by the foreign visitors, could not possibly have taken place within the confined spaces of the Royal Centre. For these reasons we have decided here to simply call the monument the Great Platform, thereby leaving the associations with the Mahanavami open to question.

If we cannot be certain about the Great Platform's original purpose, or its possible changing functions over a period spanning the 14th to 16th centuries, we may at least be confident about its architectural and artistic significance. The overall form of the platform, with its three vast masonry terraces rising one upon the other, must be considered exceptional in the history of Indian architecture, even if some of its details are familiar from contemporary temples and palaces. Indeed, nothing remotely resembling it is to be found at any other Hindu royal site. The same is also true of its carvings. The reliefs on the sloping sides of the platform illustrate a broad spectrum of Hindu courtly activities that is unmatched in the art of any other stone building of India. Sadly, we are lacking the historical data that might explain the motivations on the part of the Vijayanagara rulers for commissioning and renovating such an architecturally and artistically innovative monument. However, the platform seems consistent with what we know about the Vijayanagara phase of southern Indian history, in which long established, indigenous Hindu norms were modified by contact with newly established, imported sultanate modes. The most obvious evidence for such interchange is provided by depictions of the Central Asian Turks who were evidently employed at the Vijayanagara court. From this point of view the art of the Great Platform offers us a unique insight into a complex, multi-layered culture.

Without Dallapiccola's long-standing study of the Great Platform it would not have been possible to bring out this volume, and we are honoured to salute her scholarship and constant commitment to this project. Here, too, we should like to thank Surendra Kumar, whose photographs are reproduced here. We also gratefully acknowledge the contributions of Tandi Hufnagel and R. Kamalahasan, two talented young architects who took considerable pains to meticulously measure the four faces of the platform so as show each and every block. The final ink drawings as well as the jacket image were prepared for publication by Graham Reed.

Our work at Hampi during the 1980s and 1990s was only possible thanks to the gracious permission of the Archaeological Survey of India. We would particularly like to thank the Karnataka Department of Archaeology, which provided essential logistical support in the form of a well serviced camp, conveniently located only a short distance from the Great Platform in the middle of the Royal Centre. Funding to maintain this temporary home for visiting teams of scholars and students was provided by the Foreign Currency Program of the Smithsonian Institution, as administered by the American Institute of Indian Studies in New Delhi.

As with previous volumes in our Monograph Series we are indebted to Ramesh Jain and Siddharth Chowdhury at Manohar for conscientiously supervising the production and printing. Donations by a number of friends and colleagues have made it possible for us to bring out this particular volume. To all these individuals and institutions we offer our profound gratitude.

JOHN M. FRITZ AND GEORGE MICHELL
London, April 2009

AUTHOR'S NOTE

On a very hot and dusty day in March 1971, I arrived at Vijayanagara at the end of an extensive four week tour of southern India. My two companions and I had visited the most important artistic and cultural sites of Tamil Nadu, Kerala and Karnataka. However, nothing could prepare us for the unique setting of Vijayanagara, its extent, and its art.

I cringe inwardly recalling my complete indifference to what was before my eyes. My indifference stridently contrasted with the enthusiasm of my two companions, who were entranced by the glorious majesty of the ruins and their dramatic setting in the surrounding landscape. Eventually, we stood before the Great Platform: I remember distinctly that in order to seek respite from the glare of the late morning sun I sat in the shade beneath the banyan tree, which still stands to the south of the monument – how often I have sheltered there since that day! While there, I looked at the numerous carvings on the south face of the Great Platform, without taking real notice of them. Subconsciously, I had made the fatal error of comparing them with the sculptures of the Badami caves, which we had just visited prior to arriving at Vijayanagara. In other words, I was not impressed. I murmured to myself: 'And perhaps there will be some poor soul (I used a much stronger expression) who will eventually catalogue this junk!' I did not know, at that point, that I had had a prophetic insight, as exactly 20 years later I commenced to catalogue 'this junk'. After this first visit, I returned to Vijayanagara frequently in the early 1970s. My former husband, who had no professional interest whatsoever in Indian art but was enthusiastic about the site, always found a way during our annual visit to India to squeeze Vijayanagara into the itinerary. I, however, did not warm to the site in the least.

It was only in the spring of 1981 when George Michell came to Heidelberg, where he delivered an inspiring lecture on the work of the then newly established Vijayanagara Research Project, that my biased attitude towards the site slightly changed and I became interested in the Project. In May 1982 I visited George Michell and John M. Fritz in London and, not unexpectedly, I succumbed to their enthusiasm. As a result, I promised to convene a conference on Vijayanagara at the South Asia Institute of Heidelberg University, where I was teaching at that time. The conference, took place in July 1983 at which the work of the members of Vijayanagara Research Project was prominently featured. Along with it, Richard Blurton and Snehal Shah arranged an exhibition of photographs and drawings executed by the architectural team of the Project. As a result of my organizing, convening the conference, and the subsequent publication of the proceedings, I was invited to participate in the Project: an honour, indeed. Still I was not very sure of myself. Eventually, however, I decided to go back to the site and became committed.

I now look back to a quarter of a century of rewarding research at the site: there have been ups and downs, as it is always in life. However, despite my initial dithering and doubts, I must say that it was a memorable experience, not only from the academic but, most importantly, from the human point of view. I am grateful to George Michell and John M. Fritz for having given me this opportunity of a lifetime.

Anna L. Dallapiccola
Edinburgh, April 2009

Chapter One

PREVIOUS SCHOLARSHIP

The Great Platform is undoubtedly one of the most enigmatic monuments of India, and its study must take into consideration some 200 years of scholarship, in addition to the reports of the foreign travellers from the 15th century onwards. Firstly, this monument is know under various names: Mahanavami Dibba, Singavasanum or Takht, and Throne Platform, or simply Throne, House of Victory, or the more neutral Great Platform. Secondly, in spite of its enduring association with royal ritual, the function of this monument is by no means clear.

The visit to Vijayanagara in 1799-1800 by Colonel Colin Mackenzie, who was later to become Surveyor General of India, is of momentous importance for all subsequent research at the site. Acknowledgement must be paid to Mackenzie for his perseverance and to the ability of his documentation team, who prepared a map, the first ever for the Vijayanagara site.[1] The annotation on the engraved copy of the map referring to the Great Platform reads: 'Marnum Dibba [Mahanavami dibba] or Tukht [takht] on which the Rayeel [Raya] received the Compliments of his court on Dussera'. Presumably based on information supplied by local guides during Mackenzie's visit, this annotation links the platform, or dibba, to the Mahanavami festival, better known in those days and since as Dasara, while specifying the monument as a takht, or royal throne. The notion of a royal association must have survived the destruction of the city in 1565. The idea of the Great Platform serving as a throne is also found in an anonymous description of the site prepared at the same time as the map, in which the platform is described as 'Singavasanum or Takht of the Ancient Sovereign' (presumably the simhasana, or lion throne).[2] This notion of the platform being a royal seat recurs throughout the early scholarship on Vijayanagara. According to De Warren, who visited Vijayanagara in 1836, it was 'la place ou s'élevait le trône des rois' (De Warren 1845: 171). In the 1879 edition of *Murray's Handbook* the platform is simple called 'the Throne' (Filliozat 1999: 334). The name Mahanavami Dibba, spelt variously, is found repeatedly in the archaeological reports beginning with the *Report of the Curator of Ancient Monuments in India 1881-82* (cxxx), as well as in the map in *Annual Report of the Archaeological Survey of India, 1903-04* (pl. xxiii).

Alexander Rea, Surveyor of the Madras Survey from the mid 1880s to 1911, was the first archaeologist to attempt to correlate the ruins of the Royal Centre with the description of the palace given by Abdul Razzaq Samarqandi, the Persian envoy who visited Vijayanagara in 1443-44.[3] Razzaq calls the Great Platform the 'Maharnavami Dibba or Throne' (Rea 1886-7: 507-8). This identification, however, is problematic. Razzaq gives a fairly detailed account of the Mahanavami festival, noting the processions and the entertainments that took place in 'a vast space of land' overlooked by the king, accompanied by his retinues from 'pavilions magnificently ornamented' (Major 1992 [1857]: 36). Whether this area was within the confines of the Royal Centre or, more likely, outside the walled limits of the Urban Core, is not clear from this description. This visitor carefully describes the throne of the Vijayanagara king, which was specially set up on this occasion. He records that it was of 'extraordinary size ... made of gold and enriched with precious stones of extreme value', and 'before the throne there was a square cushion' on which the king himself sat. The throne was accommodated within a chamber with walls and roof covered with 'plates of gold inlaid, enriched with precious stones' (Major 1992 [1858]: 38).

Robert Sewell's *A Forgotten Empire*, published in 1900, contains the English translation of the chronicles of the Portuguese horse traders, Domingo Paes and Fernao Nuniz, who were at Vijayanagara in about 1520-22 and 1535 respectively. Here again the platform is associated with rites of the Mahanavami festival. However, in this case, as with Razzaq, it is difficult to correlate the accounts of these visitors with the monument itself. Paes, the most enthusiastic and detailed of the two chroniclers, specifies that the royal ceremonies of the Mahanavami took place at the king's palace. His description begins with the sequence of gateways and courts, through which he had to pass in order to arrive at a building, which stood on 'pillars shaped like elephants and with other figures, and all open in front, and they go up to it by staircases of stone; around it, underneath, is a terrace paced with very good flagstones. This house is called the House of Victory, as it was made when the king [Krishnaraya] came back from the war against Orya [Orissa]' (Sewell 1970 [1900]: 254). Presumably the roof of the building rested on columns, some of which were adorned with rearing yalis and other fabulous animals, which Paes describes as 'elephants'. Archaeological investigations have revealed the existence of column sockets on topmost terrace of the Great Platform, and it would be tempting to conclude that these are evidence for a House of Victory.

This identification is, however, questioned by a further passage in Paes' chronicle, in which he refers to two buildings 'of the same sort as the House of Victory ... served by a kind of staircase of stone beautifully wrought, one is in the middle and the other at the end, these buildings have two platforms one above the other, beautifully sculptured, with their sides well made and worked' (Sewell 1970 [1900]: 254). Paes notes that the king sat on the top of the platform in the company of his favourites, including the Portuguese envoy Christovao de Figueiredo. Paes's marvel and awe know no bounds when he reports on the shrine, adorned with plates of gold and gems, that was set up in the House of Victory, to which Krishnaraya came to worship each morning during the Mahanavami (Sewell 1970 [1900]: 254-6).[4]

Sewell and most authorities after him do not hesitate to identify the Great Platform with Paes's House of Victory, founded by Krishnaraya in commemoration of his victorious Orissa campaign in 1513-16.[5] Yet Paes clearly refers to other buildings of the 'same sort' as the House of Victory, and it is by no means clear which one of these structures might indeed correspond to the Great Platform. Nor does the chronicle of Fernao Nuniz shed further light on the problem: indeed, in his succinct account of the Mahanavami he only refers to the 'nine castles' erected for ceremonial purpose 'in a piece of ground which is in front of the palace', and the 'throne of gold and precious stones' on which the king sits on this occasion (Sewell 1970 [1900]: 357-8).[6]

Although these reports might lead one to conclude that the Mahanavami celebrations would have taken place in the proximity of the Great Platform, nothing in these accounts can be specifically related to the monument itself. Furthermore, knowing the terrain immediately around the monument, it is difficult to visualize where there would have been the space to accommodate the royal guests and the parading elephants, horses, camels and troops, not to speak of the attending crowds of onlookers. Despite these uncertainties, the literature on the Great Platform sustains the view that it was indeed used by the king on the occasion of the Mahanavami.

Yet the early scholars commenting on the sculptural friezes of the monument did not associate these carvings with the Mahanavami, even although they recognised their obvious royal iconography. At first the sculptures on the platform were compared with the Assyrian reliefs at Nineveh (Taylor and Fergusson 1866: 65-6), while another scholar states that they are 'extremely interesting' but does not elaborate further (Rea 1887: 50). The *Bellary Gazetteer* of 1904 admits that the carvings are 'the most spirited in all the ruins', and that 'these mural sculptures are unique in Southern India', but offers few further details (Francis 1904: 278).

There is a fairly detailed notice on this monument in the *Annual Report of the Archaeological*

Department, Southern Circle (1912-13: 47-8), in which, incidentally, the carvings are identified as depicting 'hunting scenes and incidents from the Ramayana'. Longhurst is the first authority to give a full account of the sculptures of the great Platform, comparing them with the processions depicted on the exterior of the enclosure wall of the Ramachandra (Hazara Rama) temple (Longhurst 1925 [1917]: 55-63). He points out that many of the scenes on the platform are in accord with the account of the Mahanavami given by Nuniz. Longhurst draws particular attention to the parades of warriors, horses and elephants, as well as the dancing-girls and musicians. Although to a certain extent true, the carvings display a number of further themes that bear no connection to the Mahanavami (e.g. hunting scenes and depictions of birds, trees and natural life). If, however, there is a correlation between the account of the Mahanavami and sculpted friezes it is to be found on the outer face of the enclosure wall of the Ramachandra temple rather than on the Great Platform itself (Verghese 2000: 224).[7]

It is doubtful whether the scenes of courtly receptions, parading of horses, camels and elephants, and various other entertainments, ranging from hunting to the performance of Central Asian dancers, sculpted on the monument, are necessarily connected to the Mahanavami festival. It is argued here that all these scenes are connected to courtly life in general, rather than to a specific and formal event such as the Mahanavami. However, while visual renderings of the Mahanavami festival remain elusive, those of another important event in the life of the city, the spring festival or Vasantotsava,[8] appear prominently on the South Staircase and Phase IV of the platform, as well as on other monuments at the site (Verghese 2000: 222-8). Verghese suggests that because the Vasantotsava was a communal event, and not a solemn, formal festivity, it readily found a place in sculpture (Verghese 2000: 224). The Vasantotsava lasted nine days, culminating with the marriage of Virupaksha and Pambambika and the chariot festival. The celebrations would involve everyone from the ruler to the populace: there was dancing, squirting coloured water, playing music and witnessing theatrical performances. This would not have been the case with the Mahanavami, where the crowds were merely spectators and not participants.

Foreign visitors who observed in detail the Mahanavami festival do not seem to have taken any notice of the Vasantotsava; perhaps they considered it to be a folkish event, not worth recording. Whatever the case the Vasantotsava would never have been an event of such relevance to which all the subordinate chiefs and grandees of the empire, and the occasional foreign guest, would have been invited. One of the few travellers, however, who seems to have witnessed the spring festival is Nicolo' de' Conti: 'There are also three other festival days during which they sprinkle all passers-by, even the king and queen themselves, with saffron water, placed for that purpose at the wayside. This is received by all with much laughter' (Sewell 1970 [1900]: 83). Nonetheless, the Vasantotsava representations attracted the attention of Longhurst, who identified them as 'Holi' festival, no doubt because of the squirting of coloured water (Longhurst 1925 [1917]: 55-63). Balasundram is the first authority to clearly distinguish between the scenes that, according to him, correspond to the Nuniz's vivid description of the Mahanavami processions that took place around the Throne Platform, and those that portray the festivities of 'Holi' (Balasundram 1941: caption inserted between 18-19). The Vasantotsava theme appears at prominent places on the monument: on the South Staircase and on the chloritic schist blocks on the west face. This emphasis on dancing, squirting and water play, leads to the possibility that this area, with its numerous water features and restricted access (see Chapter 2), may have been the locale of the king's celebrations of the Vasantotsava rather than the Mahanavami festival.

In conclusion, the carvings on the Great Platform probably do not depict the Mahanavami festival, but are a celebration of the power of the ruler: his riches are displayed in the number of elephants, horses, military personnel, household personnel and entertainers of the most diverse types, as well as women, portrayed in the reliefs. The carved friezes of the Great Platform should be perhaps evaluated along with those on the exterior walls of the Ramachandra temple. Both this temple and the platform are royal monuments, intrinsically linked with the public and ritual activities of the king. On the one hand, the ruler grants audience to foreign delegations, watches martial exercises, participates in hunting expedition and reviews the various divisions of the army. On the other hand, he relaxes while watching dance and music performances, and celebrates the Vasantotsava festival in the company of his women and courtiers.[9]

In spite of all these discussions the question that continues to remain unanswered is whether the monument now called Great Platform, is to be identified with Throne Platform or House of Victory described in such glowing terms by the 15th- and 16th-century visitors. The mystery surrounding the function of the monument endures.

NOTES

1. The original watercolour map is now in the Oriental and India Office Collection, The British Library, London, with an engraved copy dated December 1800 in the National Archives, New Delhi, F 189/3; reproduced in Filliozat and Michell (1981: 2-3).
2. *Account of the Present State of the Anegoondy Country In the Salleevahan Year of 1722 or the English Year of 1800.* Mackenzie Collection, X, p. 128, Oriental and India Office Collection, The British Library, London.
3. First available in the English translation by Major (1857). A more recent translation has been prepared by Thackston (1989).
4. For a complete quotation of Paes's account of the Mahanavami festival see Sewell (1970 [1900]: 253-68).
5. For example, Francis (1904: 268), Longhurst (1925 [1917]: 56), Balasundram (1941: 18), Devakunjari (1970: 23) and Raman (1990: 677).
6. For a complete quotation of Nuniz see Sewell (1970 [1900]: 357-60).
7. According to Verghese (2000: 223-4) the only possible sculptural renderings of the Mahanavami processions are those on the exterior face of the enclosure wall of the Ramachandra temple: 'where, vividly depicted, are five bands of friezes of courtly scenes: royal figures watching the parade of elephants, horses, soldiers, dancers and musicians. These tally with the processional arrangements of this festival as described by Paes. However, none of the religious ceremonies that took place during Mahanavami nor the mythological associations of the festival are portrayed in these friezes.'
8. Commenting on the confusion between Holi and Vasantotsava, Verghese (2000: 223) notes that Vasantotsava, or spring festival, falls on the full moon of Chaitra, April-May, whereas Holi occurs one month earlier, on the full moon of Phalguna (February-March). Furthermore, the spring festival has a long history; it was celebrated from at least the third century, while Holi became popular only during the 14th century. Although the Vasantotsava continued to exist as an independent festival, eventually, it merged with Holi. Verghese also adds that while there is no epigraphical reference to Holi, there is a wealth of literary and sculptural material relating to the Vasantotsava celebrations at Vijayanagara.
9. The spring festival was celebrated privately by the court. Vivid descriptions of pleasure gardens and pools in which members of the royal family revel occur frequently in Kannada literature of the Vijayanagara period. Works such as Kanakadasa's *Mohana Tarangini,* of the mid 16th century, and Virupaksha Pandita's *Channabasava Purana,* all have extensive sections on the Vasantotsava celebration. In the *Channabasava Purana* the spring festival festivities are part of celebration of the wedding of Shiva and Girije, i.e. Parvati.

Chapter Two

URBAN CONTEXT

The Great Platform is the most dominant feature of the Royal Centre, being elevated on a natural rocky rise that marks the highest point of this zone. Staircases on the south and west, and an entrance chamber with additional flights steps on the east, ascend to the square terrace which crowns the platform, situated some 10 m. above ground level. From here it is possible to look out over the walled enclosures and their ruined features that constitute this part of the Vijayanagara site. A brief examination of these features is necessary in order to appreciate the urban context of the monument and its relationship to the routes of movement through the Royal Centre.

The Great Platform is located in the north-east quadrant of the largest walled enclosure of the Royal Centre. *(Figure 1)* Massive walls wrap around the monument on two sides to create an artificially raised terrace on the east, and a narrower sloping ground surface on the north. The walls here are composed of roughly shaped blocks with loose joints, and are partly reconstructed; near to the north-east corner of the platform they climb over rugged boulders. The walls follow slightly curving lines; joints on the north and south faces suggest that the terrace on the east may have been extended on at least one occasion; reused sculpted blocks are incorporated into the south face of east terrace. These walls adjoin the more regularly laid out and solidly built walls that define the eastern and western boundaries of the enclosure.

The walls near to the north-west corner of the Great Platform are interrupted by a doorway opening, from which steps descend to a series of long (east-west) courts, one of which is paved. The walls here are now reduced to just a few, partly reconstructed courses. The staircase near to the platform, just noted, has a broad flight of steps flanked by balustrades with rolled ends. Yet another flight of steps, flanked by a single elephant balustrade, links the two eastern courts at the lower level. Further access is provided by entryways on the east and west. That on the east is associated with two stone doors, now displayed a short distance to the north. The doors imitate with remarkable faithfulness the panels, hinges and locks of actual wooden examples.[1]

The features just noticed appear to define a formalized and restricted access to the platform from the north. This contrasts markedly with the spaces to the south and west, within the walled enclosure, which offer what appears to be an unrestricted approach to the staircases on these sides of the monument. This zone is of interest for its numerous water features. These seem to have been serviced by an aqueduct running east-west through the eastern half of the enclosure. The aqueduct begins as a water channel cut into bedrock, develops into a plaster-lined stone trough, and continues as a stone chute elevated on posts. At its western end, the aqueduct makes two turns, and eventually peters out not far from the south-west corner of the platform

Channels run southward from this aqueduct: one supported on a rubble wall leads to the very large rectangular bath that occupies the southern part of the south-east quadrant of the enclosure; another shorter chute, carried on posts, dips downward so as to conduct water into a square pool with descending terraces and steps laid out in a strictly symmetrical manner, entirely fashioned out of grey-green chloritic schist. Letters and numbers incised onto the blocks indicate directions and courses, as if they were intended to be dismantled and then reassembled. (If such a reconstruction took place in Vijayanagara times, as generally assumed, then the blocks constituting the pool may have been brought from another site; see Wagoner 2009.) The foundations of a ruined structure faces onto the pool from the south. This consists of a square basement with column footing blocks, all in granite, in the middle of which is a small square brick chamber with a doorway defined by stone jambs on the north.

Other water features are exposed to the west of platform, in the same north-east quadrant of the enclosure. One near to the southwest corner of the monument consists of a large rectangular pool with an extension to the west, lined with superimposed sequences of stone courses on all sides. Plaster lines the floor of the pool; steps, probably replacements, are seen on the west. The pool abuts a natural boulder into which a small square cistern has been cut.

The next water feature is located to the west of the southern half of the Great Platform. This consists of a rectangular bath, with plaster lined walls on three sides and a plaster lined floor with a raised terrace on the west reached by narrow steps. Four brick stumps in the middle may have supported a central pavilion. Portions of a stone channel, ending in a chute cantilevering over the bath, are seen near to the south-west corner.

The last water features to be noticed here is a small square pool with finely finished stone sides, into which a chute runs from the north. A tripartite basement moulding continues along the south side, while a raised terrace is seen on the north. Various walls, one preserved almost to its full height according to its capping pieces, run northward into the north boundary wall of the enclosure.

Features of the north-west and south-west quadrants of the same enclosure need also to be mentioned here since they are situated only a short distance from the Great Platform. The northern boundary of the north-west quadrant is occupied by a large raised terrace, some 40 m. square, with exactly 100 (i.e., 10 by 10) stone footing blocks. Staircases on the west and south sides of the terrace appear to ascend to an upper level, now vanished. To the south of this hall is a dense and somewhat irregular cluster of rectangular basements, many with stone footing blocks, others with traces of rubble walled chambers. Here, too, is an underground chamber lined with chloritic schist slabs, and a small court paved with both limestone and schist.

The foundations of 12 long columned structures running north-south are seen in the south-west quadrant of the same enclosure. They are built close together, with only narrow passageways in between. In the extreme south of this quadrant are the remains of an aqueduct that partly follows a natural crevice.

The enclosure is surrounded by a walled alley on the east, south and west. This links the lower courts to the north of the Great Platform with the Ramachandra temple located a short distance to the north of the large terrace with the 100 column footings, just mentioned. This temple is the best preserved religious edifice in the Royal Centre. Its central location in this part of the site is emphasized by a number of roads that converge on the open space in front of its entrance gateway. Friezes depicting processions, possibly of the Mahanavami adorn the outer face of the enclosure walls that contain the temple in a rectangular compound. The walled alley at this point runs south from a small doorway in the Ramachandra temple enclosure. The alley serves as a barrier between the enclosure containing the Great Platform and similarly walled zones further to the west. These zones have been cleared to reveal a number of features, including masonry foundations of multi-level structures, termed palaces by the excavators. They are reached through complicated entryways incorporating interior courts and gateways with several changes of direction.

NOTE

1. Longhurst (1925 [1917]: 55-7) writes a detailed note on the stone door: 'Lying on the ground close under the northern wall of the platform, and formerly hidden from view by debris and bushes, was discovered the huge stone door now set up by the roadside on this side of the Throne Platform. It is a remarkable piece of work, cut (bolt-sockets and all) from a single stone, and panelled to represent a battened wooden door. There is nothing to indicate to which building it originally belonged.'

Chapter Three

ARCHITECTURAL FEATURES

George Michell

Providing the Great Platform at Vijayanagara with a coherent architectural description is by no means an easy task considering the complex nature of its built fabric. The monument has been subjected to successive phases of construction and expansion that span the whole of the Vijayanagara occupation of the Hampi site. Even pre-Vijayanagara period fragments have been discovered on and near the Great Platform: one block with an inscription going back to the 1st–2nd century CE; another with a record dated 1078; yet a third referring to the death of Jaina ascetic (*ARE* 1893-94: 545; *ARIE* 1975-76: B 94-6; *SII* V: 221; and Patil and Patil 1995: 374-5 and 377-8). But these and other limestone and chloritic schist blocks are clearly reused pieces brought from dismantled structures, most likely at distant sites, and do not form an intrinsic part of the history of the monument itself.

No data is available by which to date the building phases of the Great Platform with precision; the chronology proposed here can only be in the nature of a hypothesis. Furthermore, the present-day condition of the monument and its surrounding architectural features poses particular problems since the Archaeological Survey of India has been actively engaged in clearing and rebuilding activities on several occasions during the 20th century, most recently at the end of the 1990s. The lack of systematic excavation and follow-up publication means that it is only with difficulty that the authentic fabric of the monument can be distinguished from modern reconstruction. In spite of these limitations, the architectural observations offered here make some claim to completeness, based as they are on a detailed examination of the building's external fabric.

The Great Platform consists of three solid, superimposed granite basements, of diminishing square areas. *(Figure 2)* The topmost basement supports a square terrace, reached by access steps from the east and west. The west side of the monument is faced in grey-green chloritic schist, a material that is easily differentiated from the granite portions beneath. We propose that the basements and facing blocks belong to four successive stages of construction, here termed Phases I to IV.

PHASE I

(Figures 3 to 6)

It is argued here that the Great Platform was founded soon after the establishment of the Royal Centre, towards the middle of the 14th century. This dating, however, cannot be confirmed either by archaeological or historical data; it has been suggested by the characteristic jointing of the granite blocks and the lively carvings with which they are covered.

The granite blocks of Phase I define a somewhat irregular square basement measuring 29 m. on the east, 33.2 m. on the north, 38.5 m. on the west and 35 m. on the south, with about a 6 m. prolongation eastward from the south-east corner. (Both the original and later south-east corners are built into basement extensions.) On the north, where the ground level rises, the top of the basement is interrupted by boulders and eventually disappears. Nothing can be seen of the east face of the Phase I basement, which is doubtless buried under the earthen fill of the terrace that extends eastward from the monument. That this east face once existed is indicated by perceptible joints: two at the south-east corner of the monument, and one coinciding with the later face at the north-east corner, clearly visible on north face of the enclosure wall as seen from the lower terrace. More than half of the west face of the basement is concealed by the chloritic schist blocks of the bottom series of the mouldings of Phase IV. However, the two western corners of Phase I are plainly exposed, that at the north-west corner being distinctly shorter due to the gradual rise in ground level and the loss of the topmost course of the granite blocks.

The Phase I blocks, which are all in one plane, define a basement that tapers slightly as its rises. Up to six courses are seen in the middle of the south side, attaining a maximum height of 3.5 m. above ground level at this point, with an overall incline of about 20 to 25 cm. Here the basement is interrupted by the South Staircase. The walls bounding the staircase on its east and south sides are not contiguous with those of the basement itself (there are clear joints); for this reason the South Staircase may be considered slightly later than Phase I, though probably earlier than Phase II. (For this reason the carvings on the South Staircase are treated separately; see Chapter 7.) Indeed, it is possible that the present staircase replaces an earlier one: uncarved portions on the blocks of Phase I here indicate a flight of steps slightly different from the risers and treads of the present flight. The basement that continues eastward from the South Staircase increases in height, due to additional blocks which have been inserted here during later rebuilding. This results in a basement with an increasingly incoherent stone fabric that eventually merges with the walls that define the north-east corner of the enclosure in which the monument stands.

The tightly fitting blocks of Phase I exhibit characteristic curving and interlocking joints that are only occasionally truly horizontal. The blocks vary considerably in length, the largest measuring about 3.4 m. (south face, east part, 3.2), while the smallest are usually less than 60 cm. broad. The height of the blocks is more constant, varying from about 50 to 70 cm. The markedly irregular contours of the uppermost blocks of the basement suggest that they may not belong to the original topmost course of Phase I. Such pieces, if they had ever existed, have not been found; it is conceivable that they were removed as part of the rebuilding of the monument associated with the Phase II extension. Another aspect of the stonework worth noting is the interlocking scheme or more or less vertical and horizontal jointing. On the north face, however, the joints are somewhat curved, do doubt as a response to the natural boulders on which the monument is built, but which are now almost totally concealed.

The faces of almost all the exposed blocks of Phase I are carved with shallow reliefs in varied and lively compositions, sometimes running across the joints from one block to another (see block by block description of the carvings in Chapter 6). The variety of scenes depicted here is not matched by the carvings on the other portions of the monument. However, it is to be regretted that so many of the carved blocks on the western face are now obscured by the lower courses of Phase IV. That other blocks of Phase I were removed at various stages in the constructional history of the monument is indicated by the Phase I type reliefs set into the enclosure walls that run eastward from the south-east corner of the monument. Further detached blocks with similar reliefs found in the vicinity have been gathered into various heaps nearby.

PHASE II

(Figures 3 to 6)

This stage in the construction of the Great Platform cannot be too far removed in date from the foundation of the monument, considering the comparable sizes of the granite blocks, the jointing style and the subjects of the sculpted reliefs; even so, no precise time gap can be calculated. The Phase II extension consists of a smaller basement, also perfectly square in dimensions: 29 m. on the east, 28 m. on the north and 29.1 m. on the west. (The southern dimension is partly obscured by the Phase IV addition.) This basement is set back 1.2 to 1.5 m. from the top of Phase I, so as to create a terrace on four sides. Since the basement of Phase I is no longer evident on the east, the terrace here is extended until it meets the enclosure walls that wrap around the monument on two sides; it is partly bounded on the south by an extension of the south wall of Phase I.

The granite walls of Phase II rise approximately 1.5 to 2 m. above the terrace, except on the south where they dip down to accommodate a natural boulder that is partly sculpted. The walls are markedly less tapered than those of Phase I and the blocks are generally smaller, many of them being roughly square in shape, ranging from 50-60 to 75-80 cm. in size, Even so, some blocks are of considerable dimensions, such as the example which is 2.7 m. long on the north face (6.8). As in Phase I, the jointing is often curved and interlocking. On the west face, the Phase II blocks are partly hidden by the rubble and mortar extension that supports the chloritic schist blocks of the middle series of Phase IV (see below).

Reliefs cover most of the blocks of Phase II, especially those on the south side. Here the carving is noticeably flatter, and the compositions less vigorous but more tightly packed than those of Phase I. In spite of this stylistic divergence, there is much correspondence in subject matter (see Chapter 8). The Phase II reliefs employ raised frames on each block to define a central carved area; they are capped by a slightly projecting course sculpted with a frieze of undulating creeper. Two slightly projecting courses with somewhat similar designs are set into the walls encasing the east and south sides of the South Staircase, which is here assigned to a period somewhere in between Phases I and II.

PHASE III

(Figures 3 to 6)

The next phase in the construction of the Great Platform is strikingly different in style to its predecessors, suggesting that it is separated by a substantial interval of time from Phase II. While the date of Phase III cannot be confirmed from the available data, it is possible to compare its finely finished, deep granite mouldings with upapitha-adhishthana series on early 15th-century temples, most notably the nearby Ramachandra temple. If this stylistic correspondence is taken to imply a chronological connection, then Phases I and II would be assigned to successive dates in the 14th century, and Phase III to the early decades of the 15th century.

The mouldings of Phase III run continuously around the monument, interrupted only in the middle of the east side by the Entrance Chamber. This gives access to a double flight of steps that ascend to the topmost level of the platform. The mouldings on the west face are mostly concealed by the chloritic schist blocks of the intermediate and upper series of mouldings of Phase IV. These courses are crudely affixed to the granite courses of Phase III by rubble, bricks and debris set into thick mortar.

The mouldings of Phase III rise in two complete series, one stepped back from the other by about 50 to 53 cm. Each of the mouldings described here coincides with a separate granite course (joints are clearly visible).

Phase III, Lower Series

(Figure 7)

The overall height is 2.9 m.

Foundation (Course 1) This bottom course, somewhat roughly hewn, is most evident on the south (19 cm. high at the south-east corner), where it is set back 1.4 m. from the top edge of Phase II.

Lower Upana (Course 2) The vertical course with which this series begins has carvings of elephants and occasional figures in approximately square compartments framed by bands. The bands are sometimes replaced by pilasters, complete with shafts showing part polygonal sections, double capitals and bevelled brackets (as on the south face, east end).

Upper Upana (Course 3) This shorter uncarved upana is set back 44 cm. from the lower upana.

Padma (Course 4) This shows well formed petals (incisions on curved surface) with scalloped outlines raised on a high plain band.

Several corner petals have foliate designs; the corners are otherwise marked by upturned enlarged petals. On the west face (north end) the padma is interrupted by a small block carved with a striding figure, hands outstretched.

Pattika (Course 5) This narrow projecting band is framed by miniature, smoothly curved, padma mouldings, bottom and top.

Gala (Course 6) The highest component of this series (measuring some 58 cm.), this recessed course is divided into panels by pilasters in shallow relief. (The panels are numbered sequentially from right to left on each face, including the incomplete set that is visible on the west.) Most of the pilasters show footing blocks, shafts with double blocks separated by polygonal sections, sometimes with upper double curved sections with occasional petal motif, and double capitals (lower, disc-like elements, and upper, projecting square elements with corner bosses). Brackets have bevelled arms, but there is at least one instance of clumsily executed pushpapotika brackets (south face, between 7 and 8). The pilasters are halved at the north-east and north-west corners. The (mostly) rectangular panels defined by these pilasters are filled with relief compositions of architectural facades with varied designs set between lotuses, pots and/or hamsas; some panels are square with only a single one of these motifs (south face, 1, and east face, 9).

East Face of Gala (Course 6)

1 Pair of split-pilasters with double capitals and pushpapotika brackets, framing medallion, with fanciful foliation above, symmetrically arranged either side of a central tuft.
2 Pair of split-pilasters with double capitals and pushpapotika brackets framing doorway with shakhas and lintel block; fanciful foliation above is symmetrical arranged either side of a central tuft.
3 Pair of split-pilasters with double capitals and rolled brackets is topped by kapota with kudus either side of central blocked-out sections, top-most compressed moulding (?).
4 Same 3.
5 Pair of split-pilasters with double capitals (?) carries kapota with triple kudus, recessed kantha with bands, and kapota roof with kudus.
6 Pair of pilasters with double capitals and rolled brackets, frames a doorway with multiple shakhas containing lotus medallion; looped garlands (worn) adorn the lintel.

South Face of Gala (Course 6)

1 Pair of split pilasters with double capitals carries a pyramidal roof composition flanked by upturned petals/nagas (?).
2 Pair of split-pilasters with double capitals and compressed bevelled brackets frames a blocked-out doorway topped by high kapota, central kudu, something (?) on top.
3 Pair of split-pilasters with double capitals and compressed bevelled brackets frames a doorway with shakhas, high kapota, and a looped design (?) on top.
4 Pair of split-pilasters with double capitals but no brackets carries kapota with central block and looped design (?) on top.
5 Pair of full pilasters with compressed bevelled brackets carries a multi-lobed frame composed of tassels, with triple pendant buds.
6 Pair of full pilasters with well-articulated adhishthana footing blocks and double capitals. carries an arched torana composed of garlands and surmounted by a medallion.
7 Pair of split-pilasters with double capitals and bevelled brackets frames a doorway with single shakhas, topped by kapota with blocked-out kudus and (?).
8 Pair of split-pilasters with double capitals and brackets (?) frames a blocked-out doorway topped by kapota.
9 Pair of split-pilasters with double capitals and brackets (?) frames a blocked-out doorway (central portion damaged) with recessed kantha with bands and kapota.
10 Pair of pilasters with blocked-out doorway (partly concealed and damaged).

West Face of Gala (Course 6)

1 Top only of a pair of split-pilasters with double capitals surmounted by kapota.
2 Top only of a pair of split-pilasters, doorway lintel with central block, and fanciful foliation either side of a central, petal-like motif.
3 Top only of fanciful foliation.
4 Only the corner pilaster can be made out.

North Face of Gala (Course 6)

1 Pair of split-pilasters with double capitals and bevelled brackets framing a doorway with petalled lintel and central block containing relief lotus (24 petals?), topped by kapota with triple kudus.
2 Pair of split-pilasters with double capitals and brackets (?) frame a doorway with shakhas and lintel block containing relief hamsa; kapota with five kudus (worn) and four finials is seen above.
3 Pair of split-pilasters with brackets (?) carries upward-curved moulding with kapota showing triple pot-like motifs (?).
4 Pair of split-pilasters with double capitals and bevelled brackets frames a blocked-out doorway topped by kapota, with blocked-out central sections and double recessed kanthas with bands separated by a moulding (?).
5 Pair of split-pilasters with double capitals and brackets (?) carries a lintel with fanciful foliation and a central petal-like design.
6 Pair of split-pilasters with double capitals and rolled brackets (?), frames a blocked-out doorway with kapota with central motif (?), topped by a reduced moulding.
7 Pair of split-pilasters with double capitals and bevelled brackets frames a blocked-out doorway topped by kapota, two recessed kanthas (bands in the upper kantha) and shala with central, arch-like window and triple kalasha finials.
8 Pair of split-pilasters, with double capitals and brackets (?) frames a blocked-out doorway surmounted by kapota, two recessed kanthas, and shala with central arch-like window and triple kalasha finials (worn).

Kapota (Course 7) This overhanging, slightly undercut moulding has a petalled frieze on the underside (scalloped profile), as well as petals on the rounded shoulder (without scalloped outline). Blocked-out kudus with angled profiles are placed at intervals, almost always coinciding with the pilasters in the gala just described; additional kudus are sometimes inserted over the architectural facades (as on the north face, west end, the east face, south end, and much of the south face). A deep groove runs between the kudus on the east face (south side), south face and west face (mostly obscured). The corners are marked by upstanding, quarter circle bosses.

Kantha and Inverted Padma (Course 8) This combination of two mouldings represents the topmost course of the lower series of Phase III. The recessed kantha has shallow plain bands at the corners and above most of the kudus, while the inverted padma shows petalled incisions and scalloped outline, complete with enlarged corner petals (same as course 4, but at a slightly reduced scale).

Phase III, Upper Series
(Figure 8)

The overall height is 1.7 m.

Lower Upana (Course 9) Plain.

Upper Upana (Course 10) This plain course is higher than 9.

Padma (Course 11) This shows well formed petals incised onto the curving shoulder, with scalloped outline raised on a plain band with a deep undercut. Upturned petals mark the corners.

Tripatta Kumuda (Course 12) This outward projecting, part octagonal moulding is framed by miniature padmas on bottom and top, both with petalled incisions and scalloped profile.

Lower Kantha and Outward Bevelled Moulding (Course 13) This shows no decoration.

Kapota (Course 14) This deeply undercut moulding has a smoothly rounded shoulder (without petal incisions as in the lower kapota), interrupted by blocked-out kudus with angular profiles, more or less regularly spaced, at approximately 90 to 100 cm. intervals. Upstanding, quarter-circle bosses are seen at the corners.

Upper Kantha and Outward Bevelled Moulding (Course 15) These repeat the mouldings of course 13, but with a slightly higher, vertical edge.

Phase III, East Entrance Chamber

Measuring 2.65 m. wide, 3.85 m. deep and 3.07 m. high, this chamber is set into the middle of the east side of Phase III. As already noticed, the chamber gives access to two flights of steps that ascend to the terrace at the top of the monument. The chamber opening is framed by side walls that begin at the top of course 3. (On the outside, these walls become deeper as the basement series just described progressively recedes.) The floor level (original threshold, but modern replacement floor slabs) coincides with the top of course 3; 18 cm. square sockets cut into the upper surface of course 2, immediately in front of the walls perhaps once accommodated a frame for wooden doors.

The walls of the chamber support roof slabs (outermost slab is a modern replacement), with kantha and outward bevelled mouldings at the ends, continuing those of course 15. None of the other mouldings of either series of Phase III were intended to return onto the side walls. This is confirmed by several blocks that are carved across the corners; these show the abutment of the mouldings with the side walls.

The only internal features of the entrance chamber to be noticed here are the staircase openings at the rear (western) ends of the side (north and south) walls. Some 1.15 m. wide and 2.75 m. high, these openings are roofed with slabs carried on well formed brackets with curved profiles. The roof slabs over the steps have shallow curved sides and horizontal central sections, forming a distinctive lobed profile. As the roof slabs begin to angle upward (echoing the rise in the steps below), they are replaced by modern horizontal elements. (Carvings on the rear and side walls of the chamber as well as on the side walls of the staircase wells are described in Chapter 9.)

One of the photographs of the Great Platform published by Longhurst (1925 [1917]: fig. 20) clearly shows a cubical extension, apparently without any doorway, but with a small ventilation hole (south face), protruding outward from the entrance chamber. The extension is built upon the foundation course of the lower series of Phase III (outlines of its walls are clearly visible on the upper face), and continues upward at least as far as the terrace, if not slightly higher. From what can be judged from the photograph, the masonry fabric of this cubical extension differs markedly from that of Phase III. It is here considered to be a later addition, either contemporary with Phase IV, or possibly even an addition of the post-Vijayanagara era. That this extension was still visible in the 1960s is apparent from Devakunjari's account, which mentions 'a small chamber' that could only be reached by means of flights of steps descending from the 'floor of the platform itself' (1970: 24).

Topmost Terrace

The topmost terrace of the Great Platform is an almost perfect square, measuring some 22.0 by 22.8 m. in the east-west and north-south directions respectively. It is bounded by extremely long slabs on four sides (some almost 5 m. in length, as on the north face). Recently the terrace has been cleared by the Archaeological Survey of India to reveal granite footing blocks that are notched to receive approximately 45 cm. square columns. Evidence of burning and a total absence of any stone fragments indicate that these columns must have been of wood. But whether they were covered in precious metals or ivory and inset with gems can only be a matter of speculation. The footing blocks are arranged in four clusters defining broad central aisles, measuring 4.0 m. and 3.7 m. wide in the east-west and north-south directions respectively, with a large central bay marking the intersection. The two western clusters each consists of seven by six footing blocks (one additional row in the east-west direction); the two eastern clusters each consists of six by six footing blocks, less eight blocks in each cluster, so as to accommodate the openings in the terrace for the two fights of staircases. Not all the blocks were discovered by the excavators, and those that were uncovered were often displaced. The distances between the blocks varies considerably, from 1.2 to 1.8 m., centre to centre. (New replacement blocks have now been introduced, and the distances between them made more regular.) When first cleared, the footing blocks were set into earthen fill, but this fill has now been coated with thick concrete. A slight projection in the middle of the east side of the terrace serves as a roof extension over the same entrance chamber. There is, however, no longer any indication of the traces of rubble walls that once lined the edges of the platform, visible on the early photographs, such as that published by Sewell (1900 [1970]: opposite 269). *(Plate 1)*

It is tempting to speculate on the appearance of the columned structure that would have crowned the terrace of the Great Platform. Square mandapas with enlarged central aisles in one or more two directions the common in temple architecture at the Vijayanagara site and elsewhere. Halls in 16th-century temples commonly have rows of columns with pushpapotika brackets carrying horizontal slabs that are raised up over the central bays or aisles. The outer rows of columns are sheltered by double-curved eaves, with ornate brick and plaster parapets above; pyramidal square towers of similar construction are occasionally situated over the central bays. Whether any of these features were present in the columned structure built upon the Phase III terrace cannot be confirmed, since no reports of the architectural debris discovered in the clearing work of this part of the monument are available. As for the date of this hall, no evidence is available to indicate whether this was contemporary with the mouldings of Phase III beneath. It is certainly possible that the columned structure was a Phase IV addition dating from the time of the chloritic schist additions to the west facc, or from some other intermediate point in time.

PHASE IV

(Figures 3 to 5)

Three ascending series of chloritic schist mouldings represent the final stage of construction of the Great Platform, here termed Phase IV. These blocks are crudely affixed to the west face of the monument, partly obscuring Phases I, II and III. (Stone blocks, rubble and chipping debris, as well as bricks and mortar, are clearly visible behind the dilapidated mouldings of the middle and top series.) The considerable confusion in these sequences is explained by the incomplete nature of the component mouldings, and the obviously haphazard restoration, with numerous misplaced slabs and roughly shaped replacement pieces. Most of this work appears to have been carried out when the monument was first cleared at the turn of the 20th century, presumably after the photograph reproduced by Sewell in 1900, but before 1910, the accession date of a photograph in the Victoria and Albert Museum, London, which shows the chloritic schist mouldings that were still in situ when the monument was cleared of debris, before any restoration work. This photograph records the mortared rubble to which other chloritic schist mouldings were once affixed, but which had already fallen or were lost by this time.

Three series of chloritic schist mouldings – here termed bottom, middle and top – are easily distinguished on the west face. However, an examination of the pre-1910 photograph reveals an agglomerate of mortared brick and stone rubble extending almost to the top of the monument on this side, indicating that the Phase IV additions would have continued higher than the top series described here (coinciding roughly with the lower series of Phase III). Furthermore, there is a vertical gap of about 1.5 m. between the top of the bottom series (courses 11 to 13) and the bottom of the middle series. The considerable number of misplaced chloritic schist slabs on the monument itself and lying on the ground nearby suggests the possibility of a missing series of mouldings, possibly incorporating the courses just noted. These may have formed part of a raised terrace between the bottom and intermediate series, perhaps with plaster flooring elevated on earthen infill. According to this hypothesis the whole of the western face of the Great Platform would have been cloaked in grey-green stone, entirely concealing the earlier granite phases. Such a scheme seems both attractive and feasible, and deserves to be considered even though it cannot fully be recreated from available evidence.

Assigning a date to Phase IV is perhaps marginally easier than for the preceding phases of the monument. This is because the moulding details and niche forms found here are relatively close in form and style to those employed in temple architecture at the site. For example, a comparable design and workmanship may be observed in the upapitha of the 1554 mahamandapa extension of the Vitthala temple. They do not appear to be present in upapitha of the 1510 mahamandapa addition to the Virupaksha temple at Hampi; certainly they are absent from religious structures dating from the 15th century. If these observations are correct, then Phase IV should be assigned to the first half of the 16th century. It is tempting to identify this extension with the 'House of Victory' built in 1514 by Krishnadevaraya on his return to the capital from his triumphant campaign against Orissa, as narrated by Domingo Paes (Sewell 1970 [1900]: 254). However, the link between Phase IV of the monument and Krishnadevaraya cannot otherwise be substantiated.

Phase IV, Bottom Series
(Figure 10)

The bottom series of mouldings of Phase IV extends westward from the west face of Phase I, the blocks of which are seen to continue behind the chloritic schist slabs. The series has a pronounced central projection containing the staircase, where original schist chloritic blocks abut the (presumably earlier) granite steps. The series has been much reconstructed, and the following description is based on those portions which are structurally coherent; it does not take into account the frequent misplacements and blank replacements. The series comprises a sequence of ten courses, with an overall height of about 1.5 m.

Foundation Course (Course 1)

Lower Upana (Course 2) This course is plain.

Upper Upana (Course 3) This course is plain, with a small nib on top.

Padma (Course 4) This shows well formed incised petals with scalloped profile elevated on a plain band. Tiny flowers are carved on the petals (at north-west and south-west corners only).

Jagati (Course 5) This comprises a frieze of sculpted elephants, with occasional attendant, all proceeding toward the central staircase. A miniature petalled frieze is seen on top.

Lower Gala (Course 6) This recessed frieze shows mostly horses, with occasional attendant, as well as panels with misplaced dancers (north and south), proceeding toward the central staircase. Here, too, there are several battle scenes of particular interest (see Chapter 10).

Pattika (Course 7) This projecting band is carved with a frieze of undulating creeper motif, with miniature lines of petals with scalloped profiles at bottom and top.

Upper Gala (Course 8) This recessed frieze mostly shows female dancers and drummers, with one scene of a couple in a frame flanked by courtly women. The figures are arranged in panels separated by bands with creeper motif.

Kapota (Course 9) This shows well formed petals and jewels, with a miniature scalloped band beneath. The kudus are foliated, and one has a crouching lion. The blocks are quite mixed, especially to the south.

Misplaced Padma (Course 10) These blocks appear to be in the wrong position; possibly they belong to a wrongly assembled, reversed padma course (note lack of any clean joints, frequent application of mortar). Incised petals with the usual scalloped outline are raised on a band, carved with a frieze of stylized flowers on two blocks.

Phase IV, Bottom Series, Additional Mouldings

The sequence of mouldings just described is extended for another three courses, adding about 40 cm. to the overall height. Except possibly for the bottom upana (south of the stairway), the upper two courses of this extension are wrongly placed. They may have belonged to a series that extended upward to the level of the middle series, to which they were linked by a terrace of which nothing now remains. The upper extension mouldings are set back from the basic sequence, which they follow in overall outline, petering away at either end. For part of its length, the bottom upana sits on a granite course with a frieze of elephants (mostly defaced).

Misplaced Jagati (Course 11) North of the stairway, the jagati blocks are carved with a frieze of yalis, the animals appearing to proceed toward the central steps. (The south side cannot be seen.)

Misplaced Pattika (Course 12) This consists of a band of undulating creeper motif. A few blocks also show miniature petals on top. To the south, a mix of upanas occurs.

Misplaced Kapota (Course 13) This mostly shows petals and foliated kudus with hamsa, faced and kirttimukhas (to the north). To the south the kudus are plain. Five reused (pre Vijayanagara period) blocks at the northern end have smoothly rounded shoulder, kudus with incised hamsa, seated figure and lady with vine, and even the occasional Kannada label (see *ARIE* 1975-76: B 96, and Patil and Patil 1995: 377).

Phase IV, Middle Series, Main Sequence

(Figure 11)

The middle series sits on the uppermost granite blocks of Phase II, except for the extension in the middle containing the staircase, which is elevated on a (post-Phase II) wall of mortared granite blocks, much restored. The middle series consists of a main sequence of mouldings, interrupted by eight projecting niches (four incomplete), described separately below. Only portions of the middle series are preserved for the full height, as in the middle of the north and south sides. Elsewhere, the series is substantially rebuilt, incorporating both old and new elements. This is clearly seen at the south end, where the mouldings return around the south-west corner of Phase III, as well as on the extensions either side of the staircase, where the mouldings are simply cut off or misplaced to make way for the steps, and at the north end where the mouldings peter away altogether. (That the mouldings continued up to and around the northwest corner of Phase III, in similar fashion to the mouldings at the south-west corner, is indicated by traces of rubble, brick and mortar.) The series comprises seven courses attaining an overall height of 133 cm.

Lower Upana (Course 1) This moulding, carved in relief with a continuous line of elephants generally proceeding toward the central staircase, is set back about 30 cm. from the edge of the top course of Phase III (north and south ends).

Upper Upana (Course 2) This uncarved moulding has a short nib on top.

Padma (Course 3) This consists of incised petals with a scalloped profile raised on a frieze of stylized flowers.

Pattika (Course 4) A frieze of undulating creeper motif adorns the projecting band, with lines of miniature petals showing scalloped profiles bottom and top.

Gala (Course 5) This is enlivened with relief panels of courtly scenes separated by bands of creeper motif.

Kapota (Course 6) This has a petalled shoulder interrupted by regularly spaced, foliated kudus decorated with jewels and medallions. Narrow grooves and a line of miniature petals runs along the base. The kapota is slightly undercut on its underside.

Inverted Padma (Course 7) This has incised petals with a scalloped outline.

Note that courses 3 to 7 have shallow recesses, up to 2 cm. deep, either side of the eight niche projections.

Phase IV, Middle Series, Niche Projections

(Figure 11)

The mouldings of the middle series of Phase IV are interrupted by eight niche projections; two on each of the faces either side of the staircase (N3 and N4, S3 and S4: incompletely preserved); two on each of the faces to the north and south (N1 and N2, S1 and S2: damaged, but more or less complete). (Here, as on the top series of Phase IV, the niches are numbered inward from the north and south corners toward the central staircase.) The projections run from courses 3 to 6 of the main sequence, many of the miniature mouldings being compressed into a single course. All the elements described here have shallow central projections. (Significantly, the niches are aligned with those in the top series.)

Upapitha This consists of upana, padma with scalloped profile, and a variable set of mouldings: gala with bands interrupted by seated lions in the middle and at the corners (N3, S2 and S3); faceted kumuda between kanthas with panels of stylized lotus ornament (N1, N2 and S1); pattika with creeper motif, and gala with pots and yalis (N4 and S4). All these sequences are topped with petalled kapota with kudus near the corners.

Adhishthana This comprises padma (joint), ribbed or tripatta kumuda with prominent central band, recessed kantha with panels of stylized lotus ornament (miniature seated figure in S2), petalled kapota with foliated kudus, and double sets of tiny mouldings with inverted bevelled outlines.

Colonettes Double pairs of split colonettes (central pair projects slightly forward) show seated lions at the base, multi faceted or part rounded shafts, double capitals, leafy brackets, and pushpapotika brackets. The colonettes are cut away from the rear wall, with a central projection carved with a standing figure (at the same level as the gala of the basic sequence).

Kapota The colonettes are topped with a miniature frieze of petals, and petalled kapota with foliated kudus and kirttimukhas (joint).

Entablature Set into the kapota cornice of the main sequence (course 6), this consists of an inverted padma flanked by shallow kuta roof forms (complete with central kudus and kalasha finials), recessed kantha with plain bands (S1 and S2), and shala roof, one example with a crisscross, tile like pattern (N1, N2 and S2). The shala has a central foliated kudu topped by kirttimukha, triple kalasha finials, and arched ends with kirttimukhas at the apexes (only half shown). The ends are blank.

Phase IV, Top Series, Main Sequence

(Figure 12)

The main sequence of mouldings that constitutes the top series of Phase IV attains an overall height of 1.84 m. where fully preserved. The mouldings proceed along the west side of Phase III, set back some 68 cm. from the edge of the topmost moulding of the middle series on which it sits; the central projections are set back 2.55 m. from that of the middle series. The main sequence runs from central projections either side of the staircase to corner projections with variant mouldings (lost at the north end), described below. The mouldings are interrupted by eight niches: one each on the projections either side of the steps (N4 and S4), three each on the walls between these projections and the corner projections (N1, N2 and N3; S1, S2 and S3). In spite of the dilapidation of the mouldings and their poorly executed, often incorrect reconstruction, the original treatment of the seven courses is sufficiently clear.

Foundation (Course 1)

Upana (Course 2) This shows a shallow nib at the bottom.

Padma (Course 3) Petals, occasionally with jewelled ribs in between (either side of N1 and south of S1), are carved onto the rounded shoulder, with scalloped profile raised on a band. A tiny frieze of petals is seen on top.

Kumuda (Course 4) This multi faceted (part 16-sided), almost rounded, moulding is framed by tiny rows of petals at both the bottom and top.

Kantha and Inverted Padma (lower part of Course 5) The recessed kantha has plain bands only under pot panels; the inverted padma has a scalloped profile.

Gala (remainder of Course 5 and all of Course 6) Though mostly consisting of replacement slabs, sufficient portions of this course remain to attempt a reconstruction. The principal features are the kumbhapanjaras between full height, shallow pilasters placed either side of the niche projections. (Note the figures at the base of the gala, as well as within the niche projections.)

The kumbhapanjaras consist of pilasters standing in ribbed or smoothly curved pots with central bands, with flowing, tassel like foliation at either side (sometimes incorporating leaping yalis). Pilaster shafts are rounded or part octagonal, with double capitals, miniature leafy brackets, projecting kapotas with double kudus, kanthas with bands, and kuta like, shrine roofs or foliated panjaras, some with miniature temple towers inside, topped with kirttimukhas. The kumbhapanjara at the extreme northern end of the wall varies in some respects: the part square pot with rounded sides has flowing foliation flanked by figures; the pilaster shaft is part square with prominent adhishthana at the base.

The full height pilasters (some partly obscured by carved figures) have adhishthanas at the base (not all examples), nagabandhas on petalled blocks at the transition between the part-square and part-octagonal shafts, jewelled bands in the middle, and double curved petalled tops. Fully modelled, double capitals (part-octagonal lower elements, part square upper elements with circular petalled undersides) carry double pushpapotika brackets. These brackets appear to have been quadrupled at the corners, with two arms projecting outward.

Further features of the gala are the small shallow niches on the short walls north and south of the central projection (the north wall is lost). The incompletely preserved niche on the south wall shows pilasters with blocks alternating with polygonal sections, and part rounded colonettes at either side, framing a sculpted maiden. This composition may have been headed by an inverted padma and foliated panjara headed by a kirttimukha (lost).

Traces of flattish jambs on course 5 either side of the central staircase suggest the presence of a doorway frame. (There is, however, no indication whether these jambs would have continued higher, or if they would have supported a lintel.)

Petalled Frieze (Course 7) This comprises a line of sculpted, double curved petalled brackets, with shallow petals below. The brackets were probably symmetrically arranged either side of the niches, but only a few blocks survive in their original position.

Kapota (Course 8) This capping course is deeply undercut, with ribs and rafters on the underside. The kapota shows petals with jewels in between, and ornate foliated kudus, some with miniature faces (probably originally aligned with the shallow pilasters on the gala beneath). This scheme is interrupted by shalas coordinated with the projecting niches beneath. (The north half of the south side is wrong reconstructed; the north side has entirely disappeared.)

Phase IV, Top Series, Niche Projections
(Figure 12)

The eight niches (N1 to N4 and S1 to S4) of the top series of Phase IV run the full height from courses 2 to 8, but only niches N1, S1 and S2 survive above their upapitha and adhishthana mouldings. Each niche is provided with a shallow central projection. (As has already been noted, the niches are aligned with those of the middle series below.)

Upapitha (Courses 2 and 3) This consists of upana, padma, variable moulding (inverted padma, faceted kumuda, fluted kumuda, pattika with creeper motif) between kanthas with floral bands, and petalled kapota with foliated kudus. On niches N3, S1, S2 and S4, this scheme is interrupted by triple sets of secondary niches of diminutive proportions, complete with adhishthana, double pairs of pilasters (central pairs split), kapotas and shalas, the last with occasional crisscross designs. These secondary niches are replaced by seated yalis and figures on niche N1.

Adhishthana (Course 4, and lower part of Course 5) This consists of padma, jagati with flowers, frieze of elephants or hamsas, kantha, kumuda of different types (smoothly rounded, tripatta or ribbed, sometimes in combination), kantha repeated, petalled kapota with foliated kudus, reduced kantha and inverted padma. The uppermost two mouldings are cut by the recesses in niche S2.

Niches (remainder of Course 5) Only three examples survive, but these are badly damaged. Each consists of a narrow central recess occupied by a figure, flanked by bands and pilasters, partly cut away from the rear wall. The schemes described below are topped with a frieze of petals and line of double petalled brackets or inverted padma.

N1 A crowned figure stands inside the recess, beneath a foliated torana with a kirttimukha at the apex. The recess is flanked by three pairs of jambs and colonettes (all broken), with yalis at the base and pushpapotika brackets at the top. The well articulated brackets have pairs of side arms, or single arms shown end on.

S1 A maiden clutching a creeper stands inside the recess framed by pilasters with attached colonettes. The pilasters show square shafts, with adhishthanas at the base, blocks separated by polygonal sections, and upper blocks adorned with squatting lions and medallions. The colonettes have seated lions at the base, part-circular shafts, leafy brackets and pushpapotika brackets above. Another pair of cut-out pilasters with colonettes, probably of the same type, was positioned at either side, but only portions of the brackets with squatting lions remain.

S2 A maiden clutching a creeper stands beneath a multi-lobed frame with a kirttimkuha at the apex. The recess is flanked by triple sets of supports. The innermost of these consists of pilasters with attached colonettes. The pilasters have adhishthanas at the base and creeper motifs on the shafts, with medallions on top. The colonettes have adhishthanas and yalis at the base, part-octagonal shafts, double capitals, leafy brackets and pushapapotikas. Though broken, the outermost pairs of supports were probably of the same type. The intermediate supports show adhishthana bases, cut-out square shafts, double capitals and pushpapotikas.

Kapota and Entablature (Course 6) This comprises slightly overhanging kapota with petalled sides and foliated kudus (flowers or faces in the middle). Above this rises an outward bevelled moulding, pilastered wall with triple projections, with niches framed by split-pilasters on the projections and in the recesses, and reduced kapota.

Entablature Continued (Course 7) The entablature of kutas with kalasha finials over the side projections, and higher sequences of kapotas, kanthas and shalas, also with kalasha finials, over the central projections and side recesses.

Shala (Course 8) Positioned in the kapota cornice of the main sequence, the deeply undercut shalas have smoothly rounded sides, and central kudus containing relief temple towers or lotuses with kirttimukhas at the apexes. Three or five kalasha finials line the roof ridges; the end arches (plain) are shown side on.

Phase IV, Top Series, Corner Projections

The top series of Phase IV originally ended in part-square, chamber-like projections, each with two full walls and two short walls rising some 1.5 m. on basement mouldings. These features, which are uncoordinated with the main series of Phase IV just described, wrap around the two western corners of Phase III, the mouldings of which are seen continuing to the east. Only the southern corner projection is preserved to any extent. Of the northern example, only a fraction of the facing wall with a corner pilaster can be seen.

The pilastered walls of the south projection are raised on an adhishthana which comprises a foundation course, upana with petalled fringe, tripatta kumuda, with creeper motif on the vertical face and miniature lines of petals with scalloped profiles both bottom and top, plain kantha, petalled and jewelled kapota with foliated kudus, and inverted padma.

The walls (constituting courses 5 and 6) are plain, except for corner pilasters and two intermediate pilasters on both the west and south faces. They have part-square bases, nagabandhas on miniature adhishthanas at the transitions to part-octagonal shafts, and double-curved portions with petal motifs at the tops of the shafts. The capitals are doubled, with lower, part-octagonal elements, and upper, part-square projecting elements with circular petalled undersides. Pushpapotika brackets project outward at the corners.

The walls are overhung by an inverted padma, with the usual scalloped outline (course 7), and undercut kapota, ornamented with petals and jewels, with foliated kudus with kirttimukhas on top (course 8). Many parts of these upper courses are lost. The mass of rubble and mortar at the top gives no indication of any capping pieces.

Chapter Four

SCULPTURAL THEMES AND STYLES

The Great Platform exemplifies in its four phases the major developments of sculptural traditions at Vijayanagara, extending from the mid to late 14th century to the 16th century. On the one hand there is a strong attachment to long established forms; on the other hand there is an undeniable fascination with new forms. The local folk tradition, as seen for instance in memorial slabs commemorating the death of heroes and the self-immolation of widows, and in numerous snake-stones, had a direct bearing on the carvings on Phases I and II, dating from the second half of the 14th century and possibly the early 15th century. Here there is a preference for shallow relief carvings, disposed in bands, depicting vigorous figures in movement: marching, running, dancing. The Tamil influence that played such a determinant role in architecture at this time was also instrumental in the development of sculpture. This development, which started probably around the early 15th century, is evident in some of the sculptures on Phase III. So, for instance, shallow relief was abandoned in favour of a bolder style of carving and a less inventive layout of the composition. During the 16th century chloritic schist slabs were placed on the west face of the Great Platform, almost entirely covering the original granite bas-reliefs. The shift to this softer material allowed the artists to experiment with a more elaborate technique. The depiction of the figures lost much of its freshness and immediacy and was replaced by a formal elegance. The intricate compositional strategies that characterized the early carvings were replaced with more conventional, and on the whole simpler, layouts. The single figures, however, show an extraordinary sharp sense of observation and a love for the rendition of the minutest details.

MATERIALS

Granite is the medium commonly used by the Vijayanagara artists, and most of the reliefs on the Great Platform are carved onto granite blocks. The particular texture of this material, however, makes it prone to flaking and surface alterations (Filliozat 1985: I, 296), and this accounts for the comparative rarity of well-finished sculptures and the rendering of intricate details. As mentioned elsewhere (Dallapiccola and Verghese 1998: 7) the vast majority of the sculptures is roughly, and sometimes even crudely, executed. This, however, was not important, as the reliefs were covered with a thin layer of plaster, which enabled the artists to conceal the unevenness of the stone and improve on the details. Finally, the reliefs were painted in lively colours, though the pigments only occasionally have survived. In this course of the 16th century, chloritic schist became fashionable. Not found at the Vijayanagara site, this material was probably imported from the Gadag region (Wagoner 2007: 10). As mentioned above, the fine texture of this stone enabled the artists not only to display their virtuosity in the rendering of the minutest details of dress, hairstyle and ornaments of the figures, but also to carve projecting miniature architectural structures in which to house them.

STYLES AND TECHNIQUES

As already briefly mentioned, shallow relief is extensively used in the first two phases.

The artists were seeking to achieve a two-dimensional, almost pictorial effect in stone. This technique seems to have been used prevalently in the friezes dating from the late 14th and early 15th centuries, on the south, east, north faces and part of the west faces of the platform. The carvings are laid out in flat horizontal bands; there is no foreshortening or perspective. The human figures, trees and animals are depicted on different scales according to the role that they play in a given scene. The staircase extension on the south face of the building poses some stylistic problems. The figures are carved in a bolder relief, and the choice of themes – mythological narratives, scenes of music and dance performed exclusively by women, the celebration of the Vasantotsava – are somewhat exceptional in the overall iconographic programme on Phase I. The carving technique and style in rows 3 to 5 are more akin to that of the few deeply cut reliefs on Phase II than to that on Phase I. They are comparable in elegance and finish to the friezes decorating the outer wall of the Ramachandra temple. One wonders whether the staircase extension, obviously built along with the south wall of the platform, might have been refurbished at a later date.

A more sophisticated version of this style, using an equally bold relief, but a more controlled approach to the depiction of movement and a restricted thematic repertoire, is exemplified in the carvings of the lower upana (second course) on Phase III. A surprising return to the original shallow relief, combined with a rarified and restrained elegance informs the carvings of the gala (sixth course) on Phase III. The carvings on these mouldings are exceptional, characterized as they are by the complete absence of human figures, focusing exclusively on architectural and geometrical motifs, and age-revered themes such as the purnakumbha, the lotus in its innumerable variations, and the hamsa/mayura carrying a stalk in its beak. At the end of the 15th century and during the first half of the 16th century the shallow relief technique, once so popular, is used sparingly. It occurs mainly in decorative patterns such as the vertical bands enlivened by foliage scroll, diamond motifs or other geometrical and floral motifs, which are introduced either as partitions between scenes in the same block, or as embellishments on the basement of pillars. The artists juxtaposed shallow and bold relief techniques, achieving some dramatic effects, especially in the chloritic schist carvings on Phase IV.

DEPICTION OF FIGURES

(Plates 22, 30, 37, 40, 57 and 80)

The Vijayanagara artists of the Sangama period created a human type modelled on the images of the hero stones. Both male and female figures are characterized by robust, yet well proportioned bodies, either shown engaged in vigorous action, such as in the numerous hunting, wrestling and boxing scenes or, in majestic stillness, as the royal figures of (Phase I, south face, west part, 2.9). Female figures are shown in graceful poses as, for instance, the huntress leaning on her bow (Phase I, south face, west part, 3.3) and the stick dancers (rows 3 and 4 of South Staircase, east and south faces). They stride purposefully ahead (Phase I, south face, west part, 3.14), or aim their arrows at wild animals (South Staircase, east face, 1.1). Physical power, expressivity and immediacy are the most typical stylistic characteristics of the figures on Phase I. Although, on the whole, similar to the figures on Phase I, from which they were directly inspired, those on Phase II are carved on small sized blocks. This forced artists to create a new human type, somewhat squatter than that on Phase I. Moreover, the limitations arising from the size of the blocks compelled the sculptors to be very selective in the way they chose to depict a figure. Generally the figure is shown as if frozen in a position: either seated, standing, or riding, but rarely, if at all, engaged in strenuous activities such as hunting or dancing. As a matter of fact, there is not a single depiction of music and dance in the whole of Phase II, except for two unfinished carvings (south face, 2.14 and 2.22). Among the hunting scenes, the most convincing are the ones laid out the few large blocks (west face, north part, 6.96), or the scenes on the east face (4.90 to 4.94). Possibly influenced by artists who had come to Vijayanagara from the Tamil and

Telugu countries, a different type of human figure, more elongated and more elegant in style, was evolved in the course of the 15th century. This is exemplified by the sculptures of Phase III. This new idiom was refined to the utmost degree in the 16th century.[1] The change of medium from granite to chloritic schist implied a different technique and the opportunity of improving the 15th-century human type. 16th-century figures have relatively elongated faces and elegant and nimble bodies and are mostly shown in elegant postures, even if engaged in strenuous activities, such as in the hunting scene (Phase IV, bottom series, lower gala, north part, 6). These changes in the aesthetic perception of the human figure through the four stylistic phases are stressed by changes in fashion, hairstyle and other appurtenances.

PROFILE AND FRONTALITY

(Plates 22, 28, 69 and 94)

In Phase I human figures are shown in a variety of ways: in profile, three-quarters profile, and frontally. Particularly in this phase the main interest of the sculptors was to explore the various possibilities of depicting movement. Apart from the royal figure and the occasional nobleman seated on a throne or platform, the other figures are rarely still: they are shown dancing, wrestling, boxing, marching, riding and hunting. Most of the figures in Phases I and II are depicted with the head in profile, frontal torso, and legs in profile. There are also many examples of figures seen frontally, such as the Central Asian dancers (Phase I, south face, west part, 5.2) or the tribal hunter carrying a dead animal over his shoulders (3.3). However, the most striking examples of frontal depictions are the nine male figures boldly carved on the two bottom rows on the rear wall of the East Entrance Chamber (Phase III). In Phase IV the figures are generally shown in profile and not so often frontally. There is the occasional example of figures in three-quarters view, especially in the numerous dancing scenes. In these, often the dancers are shown turning their heads towards a person at the centre of the scene, their bodies, however, are shown frontally. Another example of figures in three-quarters profile is the couple in Phase IV (top series, gala, south of niche N1).

RELIEFS OF PHASE I

The oldest carvings on the monument are sited on the lower tier of its south face, on the south-east wall abutting to the staircase, as well as on the east extension wall. These latter two walls, however, have been pieced together during the various attempts to restore the monument, when the blocks were fitted into the wall fabric in a haphazard way. Substantial sets of carved blocks dating of the same period are on the lower tier of the west face of the building, to the north and the south side of the staircase, while the north face displays only very few, rather weathered carvings. The main themes informing the sculptural programme of Phase I are processional friezes, such as military parades with horses being shown to a nobleman or a ruler, caravans of camels, or rows of elephants at work; hunting scenes involving both courtly and tribal figures; and martial sports such as wrestling and boxing. Although there is an overall theme informing each row of carvings, the artists did not deem it necessary to follow this rule strictly. So, for instance, the second row on the south face, west part, is mainly devoted to the display of troops and marching soldiers. However, hunting scenes (2.3) or scenes of dance (2.4) intrude into the overall scheme. The same applies to the third register on the south face, west part, which is almost exclusively carved with hunting scenes. However, block 3.2 (very small and weathered) depicts two figures engaged in a conversation, perched on a high throne. Apart from these occasional exceptions, each row has a main theme which is consistently followed.

Processional Friezes

(Plates 10, 11 and 13)

The generous sizes of the blocks used in Phase I were ideally suited to accommodate carvings illustrating long processional friezes. These endless rows of animals and men are shown moving clockwise to the left, in the direction of the stairs on the west face of the monument. While the scenes depicting military parades tend to be overcrowded (south face, west part, 2.2), those showing horses being led by grooms, or elephants at work, are usually well balanced. Sculpted and unsculpted surfaces impart a distinctive rhythm to the whole register. This preoccupation with achieving a balance between carved and uncarved areas inspired the artists to be extremely imaginative in the layout of single scenes as well as complete friezes. As already mentioned, one of the main features informing sculpture in the early phases, in particular Phase I, is the sustained interest in the depiction of figures in movement. So, for instance, in the first carving on the lowermost register on the south face of the monument (Phase I, south face, west part, 2.2), the viewer is confronted with a scene depicting a nobleman mounted on a horse, his arm pointing to the left. He is surrounded by a number of attendants. One is immediately struck by the dignified stance of this minute man riding a huge, sumptuously caparisoned horse, proceeding at a slow pace. In order to stress the status of the horseman, the artist introduced a sword-bearer preceding the animal, and an attendant carrying an umbrella behind. Contrasting with the hieratic pose of this central group are two lively figures riding horses, one with a raised arm, immediately following the nobleman and his attendants. Preceding the central group are three conspicuously rendered soldiers armed with round shields and curved swords, perhaps a special military corps, and three footmen crowding the left end of the panel. This scene spills over into the next panel (2.3), where four footmen are tightly packed in the right corner. In order to suggest a larger number of men, the artist carved the figures in overlapping formation (in 'fish-scale' fashion). To enliven the scene, the sculptor oriented the heads of the various characters in different directions. Thus the sword-bearer, noblemen mounted on horse, parasol-bearer and the two horsemen concluding the panel on the right are consistently facing to the left, while the three large soldiers, instead, have their heads turned to the right. Of the three footmen sculpted at the left end of the block, two face to the left, while the last, faces right. The central group is the pivot around which all action revolves. While the general movement of the frieze follows roughly, as already noted, a right-to-left movement, the heads, but not necessarily the bodies, of the figures are variously oriented to right or left, or facing the viewer. This compositional device, which imparts an extraordinary vitality to the scenes, is consistently employed in the carvings on Phase I.

Another phenomenon which occasionally occurs in Phases I, II and III is the 'spilling over' of a scene from one block to the next, as just noted, or from a register to the one above or below. Obviously, this device did not adversely affect the aesthetic sensibility of either the artists or viewers. The case in which elements of one scene protrude in the register immediately above can be readily observed in a rather conventional parade scene carved onto the blocks of the south face (south face, west part, 2.7 to 2.9). This shows three horsemen and seven troopers armed with long spears marching towards the left (2.7). The spears protrude onto 3.10 and the following blocks. The sequence is continued in 2.8, where a horseman is depicted along with three soldiers. The scene reaches eventually its climax in 2.9, in which two horsemen, seven soldiers carrying the usual long spears, conspicuously protruding into 3.13, and two foreigners clad in flowing robes and head cloths held in place by a long strip of material, arrive in the presence of a royal figure with a chauri-bearer in attendance. There is an interesting play between the crowded portions, especially those occupied by the soldiers, and those portions which are less densely packed with figures, so as to impart a rhythmic variety to the whole sequence. The layout of the blocks depicting horses led by grooms being paraded is more predictable (south face, west part, 4.4). The same applies to the series of three camels, the first of which carries on its hump a kettledrum-player, preceded by a diminutive figure beating a small drum (south face, west part, 5.12). Each figure in these compositions has its own clearly defined space, and the balance between carved and uncarved spaces lends the tableaux a dignified, almost solemn, atmosphere. Block

4.4 depicts four horses and their grooms proceeding towards the left, the first and the last groom look towards their horses, i.e. towards the right, thus adding a left-to-right movement to the scene. The two horse-grooms in the middle face towards the left, thereby redressing the balance of movement. In 5.12 the movement clearly proceeds from right to left. This strategy of switching the movement inside a scene is frequently used in the carvings on Phase I. However, this is not the only method used by the artists in order to avoid a repetitive layout of the carvings: landscape elements such as trees of the most varied descriptions, and shrubs are introduced at appropriate points to enhance the rhythm of the composition, as well as to mark the beginning of a new phase of the action. This is evident in the four pacing elephants on the south face (west part, 6.10). The first three animals are depicted each wrapping the trunk around the stem of a tree, while the last fourth animal simply paces towards the left. Other arrangements of the compositional elements demand for a tree at either end of the composition, or for a figure in the middle of the scene, as for instance the groom, in 6.13. In this case, an elephant carrying a figure on its back is led by a groom. The group is preceded by another elephant. A tree graces either end of the block.

This formula is used in a number of other carvings (South Staircase, south face, 7.1) in which trees and grooms define the rhythm of the composition. This preoccupation with defining spaces by introducing either trees, shrubs, or human figures has motivated the artists to use also unsculpted vertical bands between one scene and the next. So, for instance, one block on the west face (south part, 4.2) is divided into four unequal parts, the largest being that which concludes the block to the left. The first three parts, roughly of the same size, accommodate Central Asian horsemen. In the first part a horseman looks over his shoulder, towards the right, while proceeding, with an unsheathed sword in his hand, towards the left. In the second part an archer mounted on a horse, turning his body against the direction of movement, aims an arrow towards right. In the third part a horseman rides on a rearing horse. Finally in the last part of this sequence, a horseman armed with a long spear kills a tiger leaping towards him. There is a constant switch of direction between the four horses, all proceeding from right to left, and the horsemen, the first two of which face to the right, and the remaining two to the left. In the last scene, the tiger leaping to the right adds yet another facet to this study of horsemen in movement by foiling the movement of the horse in the first vignette and concluding thus the sequence.

Hunting Scenes

(Plates 19 to 21, 24, 36 and 37)

Although generally the movement in the carvings is towards the west face of the monument, there are some scenes in which the direction of movement is ambiguous. This is especially the case with complex hunting sequences, generally extending over a number of blocks (south face, west part, 3.10 to 3.14), which can be viewed either beginning from 3.10 to the right, or from 3.14 to the left, and proceeding towards the right, ending with 3.10. This comparatively frequent switching of movement in a single block or in a sequence of blocks makes this row of carvings one of the most lively and interesting set of sculptures of the whole platform. The unconventional meandering layout of row 3 contrasts boldly with the remaining friezes, in which, despite the switching of movement already noted, the figures are generally arranged roughly in what seems to be a parade order. In row 3, however – and this is true for the majority of the hunting scenes of this phase – men in the heat of a hunting expedition, proceed through the forest, unleashing their dogs, chasing, wounding, and eventually killing various animals. Sometimes, the hunters themselves are chased by wild animals (as for instance in 3.7) and seek refuge on a tree. The imagination and virtuosity of the artists is demonstrated by the empathy with which the animals are rendered: gazelles peacefully grazing in a clearing; majestically strutting peacocks; jumping deer; boars sniffing the ground; tigers stealthingly emerging from behind trees or bushes, climbing trees, mauling their prey, and eventually succumbing to the spear of the hunter (west face, south part, 4.2), or being transfixed by his sword (south face, west part, 2.6 and 3.12). What makes these scenes unique in the whole repertoire of sculpture on the platform are the varieties in which movement is rendered, and in the unconventional spatial organization dictating the layout of the carvings. Although, at first sight these scenes make appear confusing and somewhat disorganized, with animals, birds, men and dogs running helter skelter on a forested background, some clear principles of composition have been consistently followed. So, for instance, fleeing animals are set on a diagonal line; animals startled by the sudden appearance of a dog or a hunter are disposed in a circular pattern, their heads face the danger they have just sensed, and their bodies are turned in the opposite direction jumping away in fear (south face, west part, 3.10, left end, and 3.13). Fierce fights between men and tigers are laid out in triangular formation, the apex of which is constituted by the heads of the figures and animals, with the hunters shown in the act of thrusting their daggers in the gaping mouth of the tigers (south face, west part, 2.6 and 3.12).

One of the most ambitious and complex hunting scene in terms of the overall monument is seen on the south face (west part, 3.1). A courtly figure accompanied by his attendant moves through a forested landscape suggested by a single tree. The man is ready to shoot his arrows at the wild animals which inhabit a clearing in the forest. His dog is unleashed and chases three fleeing gazelles. Three further gazelles jump away in the distance. This group is rendered in an ingenious manner: the three bodies overlap each other, the heads, however, are oriented one towards the left, looking towards the hunter, and the remaining two, towards the right. Although the fleeing gazelles are the most conspicuous element of the scene, being the immediate target of the hunter's arrows, a number of secondary scenes enliven both the foreground and background. So, for instance, in the foreground, near the steps that obscure part of this block, there is a tiger rearing on its hind legs, jumping on a gazelle and killing it by mauling its throat. At a short distance away, partly blocked by the abutting steps, the attendant of the hunter, armed with a sword, transfixes the hind parts of a huge boar (?). Roughly at the centre of the composition a dead animal lies on the ground, while another animal, possibly wounded, is caught by a dog which has just leaped on its back. In the foreground a dog bites the hind leg of a dying animal. While all the action is packed in the foreground, the background depicts the less gory aspects of the forest life: two male gazelles fight interlocking their horns; another gazelle scratches its nose with its hind hoof, while other animals look on peacefully. This scene is one of the few example in which the main action is surrounded by at least eight smaller scenes, each centered round its own focal point. In spite of the intricacy of its layout, the dominating figure in the scene is that of the majestic hunter, out of whose arrow this series of scenes appears to emanate. With its wealth of scenes, this block may be considered the visual counterpart of contemporary literary description of hunting sprees, packed with suspense and adventures.

Generally, however, hunting scenes are laid out according to simpler schemes. So, for instance, one block (south face, west part, 3.5) is divided into three sections: those to the right and left are each occupied by a hunter aiming an arrow at fleeing gazelles chased by dogs, at a boar and at a tiger, which are accommodated in the central and largest section of the block. Another comparable composition is seen in 3.3. This scene is divided into two sections: to the left, a beater and a hunter walk through the forest suggested by a decorative tree carved in very shallow relief, while to the right, separated by a tree, is a tribal couple dressed in leaf garments. The man carries a dead animal over the shoulders, the woman leans gracefully on her bow. The juxtaposition of urban and tribal figures is striking. A more complicated layout is seen in 3.7. This depicts various scenes divided by landscape elements, such as shrubs and a tree. The action depicted on the block can be roughly divided into three phases. Beginning from the left, the first scene shows an animated hunting scene involving a hunter, two beaters and a dog chasing a group of gazelles which flee towards a forested area represented by a shallowly carved foliage motif. In the second scene one of the hunters shoots an arrow at two gazelles while the second kills a tiger with his spear. The third scene shows both hunters perched on the top of a tree, repulsing the attacks of wild animals, and aiming their arrows at a group of wild asses and gazelles gathered in a clearing near a cross-shaped tank. Some blocks on this part of the platform, however, depict only a restricted number of figures (3.6): a beater with a dog on the leash, followed by a second dog. The rendering of the beater and his dogs here is of interest because of the juxtaposition of the deeply cut figure of the beater and the shallow carved dogs. In 3.11: a gazelle is pursued by a dog which eventually pounces on its hind parts, while another dog bites its leg. Noteworthy is the scene's diagonal layout. Both blocks are extremely striking in their utmost simplicity. The representations of wildlife on the east and south faces of the South Staircase are among the most captivating of all composition on Phase I (east face, 1.1 and 1.2). There are boars, bears rearing on their hind legs and gazelles; also clusters of animals jumping or peacefully grazing in a clearing. Finally there is an unusual representation of six gazelles neatly carved in two rows, one on top of the other (south face, 1.3). The feet of the animals on the upper row rest on a narrow ledge. A majestic boar is attacked by two dogs or is pierced by an arrow (south face, 1.3). In both scenes the rendering of the boar is has an epic grandeur. Elsewhere a leaping tiger is transfixed by the spear of a hunter (south face, 1.1); although the depiction has suffered from the ravages of time, it has lost none of its dramatic impact. Noteworthy are the rendering of dogs, especially the one which is held on the leash by a hunter, impatiently waiting to be released and jump on its prey (south face, 1.1, right end of the block). The sequence of the scenes follows roughly a right-to-left movement on both the east and south faces of the South Staircase, until the last two scenes of 1.3 on the south face where the movement is abruptly reversed.

Music and Dance
(Plates 28 and 42)

Among the most famous sculptures of the Great Platform is a composition with three Central Asian dancers (south face, west part, 5.2). Originally there were three figures, but one of these is now a mere fragment. These stout and jolly characters dance energetically at the sound of a tambourine that is beaten by one of them. Such dancers frequently occur in the context of courtly scenes and parades, especially those involving camels (south face, west part, 5.2, 5.13 and 5.14, west face, south part, 2.2, and west face, north part 2.98). Attired in what seems to be a cloak with a 'cloud collar', tied at the waist by a girdle, a ribbed, conical cap with upturned brim, and whirling long scarf, these figures are easily recognisable. At least in one instance they wear light shoes (south face, west part 5.2). Their style of dancing is energetic and forceful. The occasional awkward angles of their bodies suggest abrupt movement.[2] A break from this formal, public and ceremonial world is found on the carvings of the South Staircase. Here apart from the lowermost and the upper courses depicting mythological narratives and elephants at work, courtly receptions and horsemen respectively, the focus is on the private courtly entertainment: ladies playing and dancing for a ruler and Vasantotsava celebrations.

Music and dance are the theme of the carvings on south and east faces of the third and fourth registers. The third register is exclusively devoted to the depiction of dancers and musicians. Groups of gracefully posed female dancers perform to the accompaniment of female musicians playing the nagasvaram and mridanga. Some of the dancers perform virtuoso steps (South Staircase, south face, 3.1, 3. 2, and South Staircase, east face, 3.1). Here, a dancer bends backwards so as to touch her hair with the raised foot. In the same row a girl acrobat walks on her hands, towards a royal figure seated on a throne, her feet resting on her head (South Staircase, east face, 3.2). Sometimes musicians join in the dance, such as the mridanga-players on the South Staircase (south face, 3.1 and 3.2), or stand gracefully in a line blowing their nagasvaram and playing on the vina (South Staircase, east face, 3.1). The graceful stance of these figures is matched by the slight inclination of their heads, often in a direction opposite to that of their bodies, adding to the general impression of undulating movement. This sense of movement is perfected in the fourth row of both south and east faces of the South Staircase, where the dancers perform not in a classical style, but rather in a 'folk' style. The registers are entirely occupied by rows of kolata-dancers, stick-dancers, organized into pairs. With one hand they beat the stick of the girl opposite, and with the other hand they beat the stick of the girl behind. The elegant torsions of the bodies and the rhythms of the arm positions impart a meandering movement, occasionally interrupted by the presence of a musician enthusiastically blowing the nagasvaram.

Depictions of the Vasantotsava
(Plates 40 and 41)

The fifth row of the South Staircase (both on the south and east faces) is devoted to the depiction of the Vasantotsava. The carvings are the visual counterpart of the literary descriptions.[3] Accompanied by a mridanga- and a nagasvaram-player, a group of female revellers celebrates the spring festival. The water-sport is in full swing and the ladies armed with squirts spray coloured water on to one another (east face, 5.1 and 5.2). At regular intervals between the participants are placed big cauldrons containing coloured and perfumed water. The centre of the stage is held by Kama, the only male figure in this row, armed with a bow and probably an arrow. At his left is a female figure, possibly Rati, hanging on his arm. The attention of Kama is directed towards the lady to his immediate right, who raises her hands in a gesture of playful dismay, or perhaps surrender. The depiction of the water-sport continues on the south face of the South Staircase (5.1 and 5.2). Eleven ladies sprinkle one another with coloured water they scoop in small cups or dippers from large vats placed among them. Music is provided by a trumpet- and a mridanga-player. The compositional scheme noted above is repeated here: a sole male figure, a courtly personage, participates to the celebrations. The lady to his left, armed with a cup filled with water, embraces him. As before, the undulating movement imparted to the heads, hands and bodies of the female figures determines the layout of this register. The third, fourth and fifth rows of both faces of the South Staircase are noteworthy for their consistent and carefully planned layout, and for the sustained interest of the artists in the transformation of dance movements and rhythm into decorative patterns. These three rows are separated from the rest of the iconographic programme by two courses of decorative friezes – a creeper and hamsa design issuing from the mouth of a makara – as if to unequivocally stress their private nature.

Mythological Narratives
(Plates 35 and 36)

One of the most striking features of the Great Platform's iconographic programme, is the absence of sacred images. Apart from some depictions of ascetics in Phase II, such as Matsyendranatha (west face, north part, 5.100 and north face, 5.95), a natha on a lion (south face, 3.29), and an ascetic conversing with a woman (west face, south part, 4.5), there are no explicit religious images or mythological scenes. However, a possible exception to this rule is the lengthy representation of the life of Narasimha among the Chenchus, and his laborious courtship of Chenchu-Lakshmi, depicted on the first row of both faces of the South Staircase. This narrative is laid out on to five blocks on the lowermost registers of the two faces. The depictions focus exclusively on hunting scenes, involving tribal hunters and huntresses, dogs, boars and other wild animals. As yet it has not been possible to identify precisely the various scenes, but these sequences probably illustrate the many tests that Narasimha has to go through before winning the hand of Chenchu-Lakshmi. Interestingly, one themes occur repeatedly in this course of the narrative: Chenchu-Lakshmi leaning on her bow, or Narasimha extracting a thorn from

Chenchu-Lakshmi's foot (both on east face, 1.1, and south face, 1.2). In the latter composition, this scene is prominently placed at the centre of the register as a self-contained unit, between depiction of wild animals to the right, and a continuation of the narrative to the left.[4] Another scene which is repeated in this course of this narrative shows a hunter, possibly Narasimha, carrying a dead gazelle on his shoulders (east face, 1.1, south face, 1.1, and twice on south face, 1.3).[5] Yet another frequently recurring episode on the South Staircase is the huntress wandering in the forest, aiming her arrows at various animals (east face, 1.1 and 1.2, and south face, 1.1 to 1.3). But perhaps the most striking from an artistic point of view is the vignette depicting the huntress leaning gracefully on the bow (east face, 1.1, and south face, 1.3).[6] The phases of what is probably a continuous narration are carefully divided one form another by trees or shrubs intervening at regular intervals.

Visual Puns

(Plates 32 and 47)

Visual puns and fabulous creatures appear among the carvings of this phase: thus a man with three heads, four arms and four legs (South Staircase, south face, 5.3) and a lion with an elephant head (south face, west part, 6.11).

RELIEFS OF PHASE II

(Plates 51, 56, 58, 60 and 61)

The comparatively small size of the blocks of this phase did not permit the artists to experiment with complex layouts involving numerous figures. Most scenes display a limited number of figures up to a maximum of five (south face, 4.24). In spite of these limitations, some of the carvings executed on larger blocks are very similar in style and technique to those on Phase I. For example the sequence of hunting scenes (east face, south part, 4.90 and following, and 4.99 and following, and west face, north part, 6.96) and the boxing match (west face, north part, 6.98) all have the same grandeur of conception as the monumental tableaux on Phase I. Larger blocks appear sporadically also on the south face of the monument, especially those depicting horsemen and a hamsa frieze (south face, 6.6 and 6.8). As already mentioned, generously sized blocks appear on the west face (south part, 4.1 and north part, 6.96 to 6.100). Occasionally the scenes spread over two rows, such as the forest episode on the south face (3.7 and 3.8, spilling into 4.15.) The direction of movement on Phase II is not as clear as in the carvings on Phase I. However, on the south face it follows roughly a right-to-left direction; the same is true on the south portion of the west face. However, no determined direction is followed in the carvings on the north portion of the west face; the same applies to the two carvings on the north face. Finally, in the southern part of the east face, the movement proceeds once again from right to left. A number of blocks is framed by narrow, plain bands running along all four sides, or at the top, bottom, or vertical sides. The majority of the carvings of this phase is executed in shallow relief. There is, however, the occasional figure or scene which is deeply cut. One example is the female figure standing beneath a pointed arch, with a parrot perched on her left hand. This figure contrasts sharply with the two male figures flanking her, which are executed in the usual shallow relief (south face, 3.36). Another deeply cut figure is that of a huntress playing with her bow (south face, 2.21), and the tiny image of a soldier sporting a turban and carrying a curved dagger (south face, 2.13).

The most prominent examples of bold carving on Phase II are hewn out of a boulder placed on the landing of the stairs leading to the upper tier. These show an elephant with riders, and a severely damaged horse with rider and two male attendants (south face, 2A and 2B). The artists responsible for the carvings on Phase II were not necessarily concerned with a careful selection of themes informing each register. Most registers show a miscellaneous assemblage of representations: elephants, camels, horses, seated royal or courtly figures, wrestlers, hunters. There is, however, little space to expand into complex scenes, except perhaps the sequences on the east face of the monuments mentioned above (east face, south part,

4.90 to 4.94 and 4.97 to 4.99). The most surprising feature, as far as the choice of themes is concerned, is the appearance of ascetics and holy personages: thus, a natha seated on a lion (south face, 3.29); a seated ascetic, his knees held by a conspicuous yogapatta, and his hands resting on a staff (west face, south part, 4.5); Matsyendranath on the fish (west face, north part, 5.100); and a standing figure, probably an ascetic, carrying a bowl or a kapala (?) (west face, north part, 5.99). Matsyendranath appears also on the east face (south part, 5.95). A mysterious carving on a block on the south face (4.21) may show an ascetic in a cave. However, since the work has not been completed, the precise identification of the subject remains unclear. In spite of the haphazard combination of themes, especially on the blocks on south face of the monument, there are sections which show a remarkable thematic consistence. So, for instance, the blocks on the west face, second row on the south part and fifth row on the north part, are all occupied by studies of birds, apart from the odd scene depicting the ascetics, mentioned above, or horses (west face, north part, 5.84 and 5.85).

Depictions of Nature
(Plates 52, 55, 59 and 62)

In some blocks the attention of the artists is focused on trees: sometime a tree with lush foliage fills the whole surface (south face, 4.8 and 4.31). A tree with monkeys constitutes the theme on the west face (south part, 3.3 and 3.5, and north part, 6.100). In all these examples, the compositional elements are arranged around a tree, which is the central feature of the scene. One theme which appears only in Phase II, is the 'state horse'. The animal is shown caparisoned, occasionally garlanded, and with the royal umbrella in the background (south face, 3.11, 4.38 and 4.40). One of the most dramatic scenes in Phase II is the depiction of the enraged elephant. The animal is depicted trampling its groom, while a number of men armed with long, forked staffs try to restrain it. This scene occurs twice, it is laid out on comparatively large blocks and conspicuously placed (west face, north part, 6.97, and north face, 6.2). The scene on the north face of the monument is almost completely defaced, in contrast with the one on the west face which is in pristine condition. This gory theme is taken up again by the artists of Phases III and IV. In addition to monkeys, the 'state horse' and other horses being paraded (south face, 5.31 and 5.32), elephants, birds and other animals, one of the most striking animal representation is a splendid rendering of a jumping gazelle on the backdrop of a tree (south face, 3.35).

Courtly Activities

The royal figure dressed in the same costume as in Phase I appears frequently on phase II, generally seated and flanked by a chauri-bearer. He grants audience to traders parading horses (south face, 4.1), watches wrestling matches (south face, 4.25, 4.26 and 4.28 to 4.30, and west face, north part, 6.98), looks on to a figure on a galloping horse (south face, 3.31), or converses with a hunter (south face, 3.10). A foreign ruler talking to two men appears on the south face (3.26). This unusual theme has already occurred on Phase I (south face, west part, 4.12).

Hunting Scenes
(Plate 56)

There are not as many hunting scenes in Phase II as in Phase I. Generally, however, these scenes tend to extend over a number of blocks (south face, 3.13 to 3.20, and east face, south part, 4.99 to 4.97 and 4.90 to 4.94). The most impressive among these scenes is a sequence on the south face (4.15, extending onto 3.7 and 3.8 in the lower row), in which a man besieged by tigers perches on the top of a tree and plunges his sword into the gaping mouth of one of the animals. A striking feature of these scenes is the emphasis on the theme of a man killing a lion or a tiger (west face, south part, 4.6, 4.7 and 4.10).

Foreigners
(Plate 53)

Central Asian traders appear repeatedly, generally parading horses (south face, 4.1). On the south face, two foreigners approach a seated foreign king or courtly figure, who in turn gives them what seems to be a necklace (3.25 and 3.26). Central Asians often appear riding horses, as for instance the central figure on the south face (6.8), an obvious reference to the conspicuous number of foreign cavalry and archery troops. Riders on prancing horses, armed with swords or spears, bow and arrows, appear mainly on the south face (5.19). There are also a man armed with a spear (5.21), an archer, and men brandishing swords (4.3).

Music and Dance

Though music and dance that play a prominent role in Phase I, these themes are hardly represented in Phase II. Two unfinished carvings depict a mridanga-player (south face, 2.14) and two female dancers (south face, 2.22).

Visual Puns

(Plate 59)

These include two monkeys that appear as if they were four (south face, 2.17), an elephant and bull combined into the gajavrishabha (south face, 4.14), and the human figure with three heads, four arms and four legs (south face, 4.34). These topics appear together with fabulous creatures, such as a lion (or tiger) riding on an elephant with a peacock carved on its side (south face, 3.34).

RELIEFS OF PHASE III

(Plates 63, 64, 66 and 74 to 79)

The carvings of this phase represent a remarkable departure from the aesthetic criteria that inform Phases I and II. The blocks in the second row on Phase III are roughly all of the same size. They have a narrow plain frame running along the edges, and all of them are divided into smaller panels, separated one from the other by miniature pilasters or plain vertical bands. The only exception to this carefully planned series of blocks is on the south face (2.6), in which there is no division between the vignettes, and no plain frame runs along the four sides of the block as is the case in the others. The figures carved in bold relief, have lost the spontaneity and the expressionism typical of Phases I and II, which is now replaced by careful layout and refined elegance. Compared to the previous two phases, the variety of themes is dramatically reduced. The focus here is decidedly on courtly imagery, although the royal figure does not appear. Elephants are a common theme: pacing elephants, tied to a chain (south face, 2.5 and 2.6), uprooting trees or shrubs (south face, 2.1 and 2.6), and grasping a man with its trunk (south face, 2.3). There are armed riders (south face, 2.2), dancers and musicians (east face, 2.6) and Central Asian dancers (east face, 2.4, and north face, 2.5), as well as a wrestling scene (north face, 2.1), a chowkidar leaning on his long staff (north face, 2.2) and a lady carrying an arati tray (east face, 2.1). Somewhat surprisingly, the motif of the huntress gracefully poised with her bow appears twice (east face, 2.6, and north face, 2.5). The obsessive symmetry which governs the layout of the sculptures within a block and the restricted thematic repertoire continues onto the gala (course 6) on Phase III. Here the artists have devised an unusual decoration in shallow relief, based on an even more restricted number of themes: architectural facade, hamsa/mayura carrying a lotus stalk in the beak, the purnakumbha, and variations on the lotus motif, from the simplest eight-petalled to the 24-four petalled flower. Occasionally the lotus is inscribed in a simple square or a set of rotating squares. There are no representations of human figures. A trio of carvings is sometimes framed between two pilasters, such as purnakumbha, architectural facade and hamsa/mayura (east face, 6.1 north end), or lotus motif, architectural facade and lotus motif (east face, 6.2). However, at the south-east corner this well ordered sequence is interrupted. Here each motif is framed between two pilasters.

East Entrance Chamber

(Plates 67 to 73)

This restrained decoration on the outer faces of the monument contrasts sharply with the varied array of reliefs which decorate the East Entrance Chamber. The main set of sculptures is arranged in four rows on its rear (western) wall. Other carvings are on its side (north and south) walls, as well as on the west wall of the staircases that lead to the top of the platform. A number of themes which appear in Phases I and II, and which have been omitted in the decoration of the exterior of the monument in Phase III, appear here again in a refined form. The two lowermost rows of carvings on the rear wall of the East Entrance Chamber show a total of nine, relatively large, male figures carved in bold relief on a plain background. All of them are Central Asian, with conspicuous pigtails, dressed in their typical clothes and distinctive hats. The lower five figures, locally worshipped as the five Pandavas, depict a dancer between tambourine players. This lively trio is flanked on either side by a chowkidar leaning on his staff. The dancers and the musicians with their angular, jerky movements are the focus of the two lower rows. The tilted stance of both the chowkidars is a perfect foil to the performers. The second row shows four figures: the two in the middle may be soldiers, one of whom rests his hand on the head of a cockerel. The figures at either end are chowkidars. The stance of all four complements the movements of the five figures on the first row below. The upper two rows show a very refined version of themes drawn from the repertoire of Phase I. In contrast to the lower registers carved on a plain background, the artists took great care in setting their deeply cut figures on elaborate backdrops of trees and shrubs delicately carved in shallow relief. This juxtaposition of different carving techniques is not seen elsewhere on the platform.

The scenes of the third row depict an elephant and a groom, a foreign hunter with a spear and shield encountering a growling tiger leaping at him from behind a tree, a foreigner carrying a pole across his shoulders (the sole instance of this theme on the monument), and finally an elephant carrying a monkey (?) on its back wrapping his trunk around a tree. A stylistic peculiarity of the carvings of the first three rows is the presence of a narrow 'ledge' beneath the feet of the majority of the figures. The 'ledge' appears sporadically in the carvings on Phase I, but here is consistently used. The fourth row is divided into three panels by thin plain vertical bands. The first and the third panel show the same theme: a kettledrum-player on a camel led by a Central Asian groom and a chowkidar leaning on his staff. In the central panel, a majestic elephant carrying two riders uproots shrubs. Further figures are seen on the side walls of the East Entrance Chamber. They include a foreign trader parading two horses, a trio of Central Asian dancers, and local chowkidars. The striking feature of these carvings is the almost obsessive rendition of foreigners engaged in the most varied activities. The foreign presence must have been of vital importance in the life of the capital judging from the prominent place accorded to this splendid set of reliefs.

Birds and variations on the theme of bird and foliage decorate the western wall of the staircases. It should be noted that here again there is the use of the 'ledge' motif, on which some of the birds rest.

RELIEFS OF PHASE IV

The reliefs of Phase IV, which are restricted to the western face of the platform, are the most elaborately finished of all carvings on the monument. If Phase III marked a stylistic departure from the previous ones, the work informing Phase IV shows a complete change in technique and style. This, as noted above, is due to the use of chloritic schist rather than brittle granite. Instead of the angular, expressionistic and shallow forms typical of Phases I and II, the carvings on Phase IV display a marked predilection for rounded, elegantly finished, highly decorated and deeply carved forms. Instead of the feeling of monumentality conveyed, for instance, by the carvings on Phase I on the south face of the monument, those on Phase IV, albeit in its fragmentary state, reveal a jewel-like refinement and love of detail; they are the work of a miniaturist working in stone. There could not be stronger stylistic contrast between the immediacy and vitality of the early carvings of, for instance, Phase I (west face), and the abutting the exquisitely refined blocks of Phase IV. Specific themes have been allotted to each moulding. However, since this part of the monument has been severely disturbed, some blocks were either lost or destroyed. When the monument was reconstructed in the course of the 20th century, the occasional block was inevitably misplaced.

Bottom Series, Jagati (Course 5)

This course is entirely devoted to the depiction of elephants. The animals converge inwards towards the staircase from both the south and the north corners of the platform. Decorated variously with caparisons, chains with bells around their sides, bellies and necks, and elegantly embroidered cloths above their heads, the animals are depicted engaging in various activities, such as uprooting trees or shrubs, parading, being tied to the trunk of a tree by a groom (north part, 9). Other animals, in a riotous mood, are restrained by grooms wielding long, forked staffs (north part, 19), or an elephant crook (north part, 14). One elephants look playfully over its shoulders (north part, 8), or stares angrily at its mahout tying its leg to the trunk of a tree (north part, 9). Of particular interest is a block on the north part (1), which is carved with a numeral in Telugu script. This probably belonged to the stepped tank that is located a short distance away to the south-west. This discarded block was probably inserted here during the various phases of reconstruction of the west face of the monument (see Wagoner 2010).

Bottom Series, Lower Gala (Course 6)
(Plates 80 and 81)

Horses and martial scenes constitute the main themes of this course. However, during the reconstruction of this part of the monument some blocks belonging probably to the upper gala (course 8) have been inserted here. These are two granite panels to the north of the staircase (north part, 18 and 19). The first panel shows a dance scene, and the second panel two horses proceeding towards to the left, even though the direction of movement in all the other blocks here follows strictly a left-to-right movement. To the south of the staircase are three fragments depicting a dance and music scene, and the celebration of the Vasantotsava (south part, 4, 14 and 16). The remaining blocks of this course show parading horses led by foreign or local grooms. An exceptionally fine block is seen to the north of the staircase (6). The scene depicts a tiger hunt. Here a courtly figure riding on a horse, accompanied by a retinue of soldiers and parasol-bearer, stabs a tiger in the neck with a long spear while the tiger attacks an elephant and clings onto its trunk. At the same time, a diminutive man kneels between the elephant and the tiger, plunging its dagger in the feline's entrails. Another noteworthy scene, in spite its dilapidated state, is constituted by three blocks south of the staircase (17, 18 and 19). These fragments depict an army of footmen equipped with round shields, swords of various types and daggers. They follow what must have been a royal figure mounted on a horse. In both scenes are vestiges of parasols and fragments of a rider, while the troops have mostly disappeared. The conspicuous placement of this scene may refer to an important battle fought at the beginning of the 16th century, possibly to the Udayagiri battle of 1514. The similarity between this particular scene and the stucco rendering of a battle on the western face of the eastern gopura of the Krishna temple has already been noted elsewhere (Dallapiccola and Verghese 1998: 94). The martial imagery continues on the following blocks. Horses are led by men wielding swords. The last figure in the block abutting the staircase is that of a rider trampling upon a supine warrior. Here, too, the horses have been rendered with great sensitivity and attention to every detail of the trappings, saddles and decorations. Some animals are depicted majestically pacing (north part 5); others are shown rearing while a groom tries to restrain them (north part, 14). Another noteworthy detail is the care with which the artists have rendered the figures and their various ethnic backgrounds (Central Asians on north part 9 and 11; local soldier and groom on north part, 13 and 14).

Bottom Series, Upper Gala (Course 8)
(Plates 82 and 83)

Only the north part of this course has survived, and it is not certain that these have been placed in the original order at the time of the reconstruction of this part of the monument. The theme informing this series of panels is the private recreations of the court: music, dance and, most importantly, the celebration of the Vasantotsava. One of the most striking panels shows a courtly couple is shown embracing within a pavilion (9). This is one of the very rare depictions of lovers on the monument, and indeed at the whole Vijayanagara site. To the left and right of the couple are respectively three and six female attendants. The attendants to the right carry various appurtenances of a nobleman, such as the sword, fly-whisk and pouch for betel-leaves and nuts. The objects carried by the attendants to the left cannot be satisfactorily identified; however, two of the figures seem to have daggers stuck in their girdles. Dancers on this course are variously depicted. Some carry in their raised hands a cup or a scoop, presumably for coloured water (19 and 20), or are places beside huge vats, presumably also for coloured water (10). A lively rendering of a male trumpeter and a mridanga-player are the sole depictions of musicians on this course (13). A somewhat mysterious panel depicts a bearded man clad in a short lower garment, raising both hands above his head (14). Although his stance with flexed legs recalls that of a dancer, he has long flowing hair, similar to that of a yogi. This block, however, might have been added as an afterthought at a later stage.

Middle Series, Lower Upana (Course 1)
(Plates 84 and 85)

Similarly to the jagati of the bottom series, this course is exclusively devoted to the depiction of elephants. The animals are shown pacing, at work and together with their grooms. The same care in the rendition of ornaments and trappings that was noted above also applies here. A noteworthy scene is south of the staircase, in which two animals cross their tusks (16). There are, however, more dramatic scenes. In one an elephant grabs a groom by the waist under the eyes of two courtly figures (south part, 15). In a second scene, an elephant having caught a person smashes its head on the ground (north part, 10). In yet a third scene an enraged elephant tramples on a supine man, while two grooms desperately try to restrain it with forked staffs (north part, 11). This last theme has been already noted in the carvings on Phases I and III. The recurring theme is, however, that of elephants uprooting trees under the supervision of grooms (as in south part, 9).

Middle Series, Gala (Course 5)
(Plates 86 to 90)

The principal themes depicted in this course are courtly amusements, reception, dance and music. Most of the scenes are separated from the following by a vertical band with either floral or foliage scrolls executed in shallow carving. This course is interrupted by eight projecting niches, four on either side of the stairs. Each of these housed a central figure with subsidiary figures carved almost in the round. Most of them have been reduced to fragments or have completely disappeared, except in two examples (niches N1 and N2) which represent subsidiary male figures, probably chowkidars, flanking a central figure in the niche. Their strikingly individual traits and unconventional stances suggest that they may represent actual persons. The carvings on the blocks between projections show female dancers, musicians, Central Asian dancers and Vasantotsava celebrations. Among the numerous carvings depicting music and dance there are a few exceptional scenes (north part, 2). Noteworthy here is the immediacy and liveliness with which the group of musicians at the right end of this composition is rendered: these are a male cymbals, mridanga- and nagasvaram-players, and a lady playing the vina. The most fascinating among the dance panels is that on the north part (5). The central scene here depicts four dancing girls, including an instructor choreographing the show. Apart from its undisputable aesthetic qualities, this panel is one of the very few still bearing traces of plaster and vestiges of painting (left eye of the dancing instructor). At the right end of this course are some of the most notable reception scenes. A seated courtly figure is greeted by four men wearing a kullayi (south part, 9). Behind him are three female attendants bearing a fly-whisk, a casket or pouch for betel nuts, and a sword. Another block shows a second courtly reception (south part, 12). Here a standing courtly figure, dressed in a jacket, billowing scarf on his left shoulder and kullayi, welcomes three men standing respectfully with hands folded in anjali mudra.

Top Series, Gala (Courses 5-6)
(Plates 91 to 94)

A progressive refinement in workmanship and in sculptural style becomes apparent when comparing the relatively simple compositions informing the lower series of Phase IV with the more elaborate middle series and top series. In their pristine state the courses described here must have been one of the great artistic achievements of Vijayanagara sculpture. The few extant fragments bespeak of an unrivalled mastery of both medium and technique. From the still comparatively squat figures noted in the bottom series, with the exceptions of those on the upper gala – for example, in the scene depicting a courtly couple and their entourage, which may have been misplaced – a new type of human figure was evolved in this course of a relatively brief time span. The new 'ideal' figure was more elongated and sensuous. The first appearance of this new type is visible in the numerous figures of dancers of the middle series (for example, course 5, north part, 5). This ideal appears, refined and perfected in the figures decorating the gala and the projections of the top series. As already mentioned, not much has survived of the sculptures of this phase; even so, the extant vestiges are enough to give an idea of the new stylistic development. Due to the paucity of surviving material it is difficult to determine what was the predominant theme of this part of Phase IV. Recurring themes are the gracefully poised female figures (south part, niche S2 and gala between niches S1 and S2), one of which is a latasundari leaning on a decoratively rendered creeper. There is yet another female figure sculpted on a block inserted in the wall between niches S3 and S4. Other noteworthy figures are on the north part of the gala. Among the most impressive is that of a chowkidar leaning on his long staff flanking the kumbhapanjara north of niche N1. Another striking tableau to the south of niche N1 shows a courtly couple, with the man gently lifting the chin of a lady. A block depicting a seated courtly figure has been inserted in the south part of the gala, where niche S3 would have originally been inserted. Judging from the extant fragments it is possible to surmise that the one of the themes informing the sculpture of at least part of this section of the monument was the depiction of courtly life.

NOTES

1. The brass images of Krishnadevaraya and his queens in the Shri Venkateshvara temple, Tirumala, are a good example of the 16th-century human type.
2. The striking similarity of these figures with those in some 15th-century Islamic manuscripts, such as Hazine 2153 (f. 34 b) of the Topkapu Saray-Museum, Istanbul, and their frequent appearance in sculpture, suggests that there was a significant presence of Central Asians at the capital and highlights the cultural links between Central Asia and Vijayanagara. Connections with the Islamic world come as no surprise. It is a well known that Devaraya II (1424-46) introduced reforms in his troops and employed Muslims, especially in the cavalry and archery contingents. The strong cultural connections between Vijayanagara and the courtly culture of the Deccan have been highlighted in recent articles by Wagoner (1996 and 2000).
3. According to Kanakadasa's *Mohana Tarangini*, XIV, 47-67 (Kotraiah and Dallapiccola 2003: 87): 'The queen sprinkled coloured water and sandal paste mixed with water on the king and on her companions. He, and others as well, reciprocated to the general merriment of all present. After some water squirting, the two queens were asked to stand together with their youthful and attractive ladies-in-waiting in two rows facing each other. At a given signal the two groups started spraying one another. They held gold vessels and

syringes filled with coloured and fragrant water. They competed against each other keenly, amid great mirth and loud cheering. Percussion instruments and conches were played loudly throughout.'

4. The theme of Narasimha extracting a thorn from Chenchu-Lakshmi's foot appears unexpectedly in Phase I (west face, south part, 5.3) in rather unusual surroundings: a caravan of camels. Placed at a very prominent position, the scene is carved in bold relief so as to stand out among less emphatically sculpted camels, grooms and trees. Yet another episode of the narrative is depicted in the adjacent block (5.2) where Narasimha carries a dead gazelle on his shoulders.
5. This theme is also seen in Phase I (south face, west part, 3.3). A possible explanation for its appearance here is the juxtaposition of courtly and tribal hunters. In this context Narasimha is followed by Chenchu-Lakshmi. Both are shown as leaf-clad, tribal figures.
6. Narasimha extracting the thorn from Chenchu-Lakshmi's foot, and the huntress leaning on the bow, are themes that were incorporated into the repertoire of sculptors. They appear repeatedly on column blocks in later monuments.

Chapter Five

SCULPTURAL ICONOGRAPHY

ROYAL FIGURE AND COURTIERS

(Plates 26, 30, 89 and 90)

The royal figure is depicted in numerous carvings on Phases I (south face, west part, 2.5 and 2.9, and II (south face, 4.1, 4.26 and 4.28), and also the South Staircase (east face, 7.1). He is generally clad in a short lower garment ending above the knee, with a yajnopavita conspicuously displayed on his bare chest. Necklaces, earrings, armlets, bracelets and anklets complete the attire. Occasionally this figure sports beard and moustache. The long hair is tied in a large bun resting on the nape of the neck. A thin band or fillet worn around the head keeps the hair in place. The attire of the royal hunter (Phase I, south face, west part, 3.1) deserves special attention since it is one of the most detailed depictions of male costume on Phases I and II. He wears a knee-length lower garment, tied at the waist in elegant small pleats forming a fan at the front. A dagger with an elaborate hilt is stuck in his girdle. This attire is completed by earrings, two different kinds of necklaces, armlets and bracelets. The hair is tied in a bun at the back of the head, kept in place by the band worn around the head. The hunter also sports a triangular beard and conspicuous drooping moustache.

In the carvings on Phase II there is no evidence either of the long scarf thrown over one arm, forming a loop near the left shoulder, a sign of royalty, or of the tall kullayi. However, both these attributes appear in the sculptural art of mid-15th century monuments elsewhere at the site.[1] This suggests that the carvings were probably executed at an earlier date. In the 16th century, however, the scarf is worn by the king and also by dignitaries and other eminent persons at the court.[2] As shown in the sculptures on Phase IV (middle series, gala, south part, 9 and 12), the scarf appears to have been first wound around the waist, and then thrown over the arm in such a way as to form a large loop held at the crook of the left elbow.

The scarf and kullayi both appear consistently on Phase IV, along with the high-necked, full-sleeved, fitted tunic (kabayi) or jacket, which is a typical 16th-century item of fashion. It is either waist-length or full-length; it has no collar and is buttoned down the front (Phase IV, middle series, gala, south part, 9 and 12).[3]

The fashion conscious 16th century also brings a greater variety of lower garments, ranging from knee-length to ankle-length. This lower garment is generally draped like a lungi; however, it can be tied in a more elaborate fashion, like a dhoti. The lower garment is generally enhanced by a broad girdle or sash 'tied very tightly in many folds',[4] which sometimes encircles not only the waist but also the hips. A good example of a sash with folds is illustrated in Phase IV (middle series, gala, south part, 9); sashes without folds are also seen here, as well as in niche S2 on the same course. Wide trousers and a long tunic with a scarf tied around the waist seem also to have been fashionable (niche S2).

Although 16th-century literature such as Kanakadasa's, *Mohana Tarangini* testifies to the existence of an extensive array of ornaments worn by men, the sculptures on Phase IV yield only limited evidence.[5] Among the few items depicted are the large, round earrings worn by the majority of male figures, and the pendeya worn by noblemen and royalty (middle series, gala, south part, 9).

Little knowledge about footwear is to be gleaned from the sculptures. Although literary sources refer repeatedly to gem-studded, golden or silver sandals worn by royalty no such footwear can be detected in the sculptures.[6&7] According to Domingo Paes, however, the court custom seems to have been barefoot.[8]

ROYAL INSIGNIAS

(Plates 16, 26, 30, 42, 55 and 80)

A chauri-bearer is regularly depicted standing behind the royal figure in the carvings on Phases I and II. On the South Staircase (east face, 3.3) the male chauri-bearer is replaced by two female attendants carrying chauris and royal swords. This is explained by the fact that this register depicts the women of the king, and, in this particular case, a female retinue is appropriate. In the carvings on Phase IV the female retinue of the royal figure appears in the form of an embracing couple or a courtly reception (bottom series, upper gala, north part, 9 and middle series, gala, south part, 9). In both cases the chauri- and the sword-bearer are shown in the presence of the ruler or noblemen. Apart from chauri- and sword-bearers, the retinue includes a number of other women carrying different appurtenances.

The umbrella of state, another important insignia of royalty, held either by a lesser noble or a groom above the head of an important personage, appears repeatedly (Phase I, south face, west part, 2.2 and Phase IV, bottom series, lower gala, north part, 6, depicting a tiger hunt, and south part, fragment of 17 depicting a battle scene). The umbrella of state shading the royal horse appears in the carvings on Phase II (south face, 3.11, 4.38 and 4.40).

SOLDIERS

(Plates 12, 13 and 81)

Although soldiers occur in considerable number in the carvings on Phase I, the weathered state of the panels makes it difficult to discern their different costumes. Some of the troops wear short lower garments; their chest and arms seem to be bare and the hair, as usual, is tied in a large bun resting on the nape of the neck. Generally they wear little jewellery. Their weapons consist occasionally of long spears (south face, west part, 2.7 and 2.9), and they have daggers stuck in their belts. There are also soldiers belonging to another corps. These are generally sturdier and are armed with round shields and slightly curved swords. Although they wear an attire similar to that described above, their headgear looks like a turban (Phase I, south face, west part, 2.2 and 4.3 and Phase II, south face, 2.13).[9] The appearance of the soldiers in Phase IV is markedly different from that of the previous phases. The figures are elongated, more muscular and athletic. Often they sport a large round shield decorated with a floral motif at the centre. Some of the troops wear a helmet; others wear their hair tied in a topknot (bottom series, lower gala, south part, 17-19).

FOREIGNERS

(Plates 18, 21, 28, 31, 53, 68, 70 to 73 and 88)

Warriors mounted on horses, armed with sword or spears appear prominently in Phase I and (south face, west part, 4.1, 4.2 and 4.10) and Phase II (south face, 4.3). These are generally Central Asian figures wearing outlandish clothes such as trousers, jackets and, above all, apart from the occasional pigtail, different types of headgear. No two figures are exactly alike. However, the detail of the horses' trappings and the costumes worn by the men of the cavalry, so painstakingly described by Paes and other eye-witnesses, are difficult to discern in the weathered sculptures.[10] Elegant figures of archers riding on horses appear occasionally in Phase I (west face, south part, 4.2) and Phase II (south face, 5.21).

Apart from the warriors described above, foreigners of diverse nationalities occur in great number in the carvings of the first three phases of the monument.[11] They are generally clad in long coats, with sleeves covering the hands (Phase I, south face, west part, 2.9). Invariably they are portrayed with small, triangular beards and conspicuous moustaches, as for instance in the male figures depicted on the rear wall of the East Entrance Chamber. They wear a number of different types of hats, such as round caps with upturned brims, as in the Central Asian dancers (Phase I, south face, west part,

5.2), or ribbed conical caps with or without central knob, as in the dancer and tambourine player in the East Entrance Chamber (rear wall, bottom row).Tiered caps are also seen, as in that worn by the man leading a camel in the East Entrance Chamber (rear wall, top row). Finely pleated turbans are also seen, as in the horse groom or trader (Phase IV, bottom series, lower gala, north part, 11). This variety of headgears indicates the various nationalities of the wearers, all of whom probably came from Central and Western Asia. A careful examination of their costumes also reveals some subtle differences. Apart from the long-sleeved cloak, some of these foreign visitors wear trousers, various types of jackets (Phase I, south face, west part 4.10 and west face, south part, 4.2), and occasionally slippers with upturned points (Phase I, south face, west part, 5.2) or riding boots (e.g., East Entrance Chamber, second row, second figure from the left). The horse trader in the East Entrance Chamber (south wall) is shown as a tall man with a triangular beard wearing a heavy long cloak and ribbed conical cap.

One of the finest depictions of foreigner male dancers is that found on Phase I (south face, west part, 5.2). This composition is undoubtedly the clearest rendering of this theme. The costume worn by these bearded figures consists of a cap, which may either be pointed or ribbed with upturned brim. They are dressed in a wide, shirt-like lower garment and full-sleeved jacket with large lapels or shoulder pieces 'cloud collar', and wear slippers. One of the essential props of these dancers is a long scarf. The trio of spirited dancer flanked by tambourine players occurs repeatedly at various places on the monument (Phase I, south face, west part, 5.10 and 5.13, west face, south part, 2.2, and north part 2.98, and East Entrance Chamber, west wall, bottom row). In the course of time these depictions of Central Asian dancers were Indianized. An example of this transformation can be seen in Phase IV (middle series, gala, north part, 5). The figures of the dancer and the tambourine players also coalesced to became the 'folk dancer', one of the most characteristic and ubiquitous figures in Vijayanagara sculpture. No longer as sturdy as the original Central Asian dancer, this figure carries one or two fly-whisks instead of the long scarf, or plays the tambourine while dancing; the headgear becomes taller, tiered and tapering at the top.

An exceptional depiction carved on Phase I shows a foreign ruler, seated cross-legged on a high throne (south face, west part, 4.12). His headgear and the long pigtail (?) issuing from it suggest a Central Asian personage. Another depiction of a foreign ruler dressed in flowing robes and wearing a tiered headgear appears in Phase II (south face, 3.26).

WRESTLERS AND BOXERS

(Plates 26, 27 and 54)

Wrestlers are generally clad in short lower garments and wear closely cropped hair, or what seems to be a cap with ear-flaps. They are generally depicted in almost acrobatic poses, with intertwined bodies (Phase II, south face, 3.22, 3.23, 4.29 and 4.30 and Phase III, north face, 2.1). There are only two scenes of boxing (Phase I, south face, west part, 2.3 and Phase II, west face, north part, 6.98). Here two massive men, clad in the exactly same way as wrestlers, are engaged in a match in front of a seated courtly figure.

GROOMS, CHAURI-BEARERS AND CHOWKIDARS

(Plates 17, 30, 84 and 94)

Local horse-grooms wear the typical knee-length, lower garment, and usually jewellery; their hair is tied in a bun at the back of their heads. The same attire is worn by mahouts and chauri-bearers. Elephant-grooms in the carvings on Phase IV, however, wear the same short lower garment as in the previous phases, but their hair is either tied in a top knot (bottom Series, jagati, north part, 19), or they wear a pointed cap with ear-flaps (middle Series, lower upana, south part, 9). These figures are generally armed with a long, two-pronged staff.

The chauri-bearer, carrying the conspicuous fly-whisk in the right hand, is always shown standing behind the seated royal figure. He is dressed in a short, lower garment and wears the hair tied in a knot at the nape of the neck (Phase I, south face, west part, 2.9, and Phase II, south face, 4.2).

A recurring figure is that of the 'master of ceremonies'. While mostly foreigners are depicted as chowkidars, local people seem to have been employed as household supervisors. In Phases I and II the costume of these characters is similar to that described above for the grooms and chauri-bearers (Phase I, south face, west part, 2.5).

The chowkidars on Phases I, II and III are mostly foreigners. However in Phase IV, among the fragments of the top series gala are some figures which probably represent local chowkidars. One such figure north of niche N1 wears a tall kullayi, billowing scarf and long lower garment is shown leaning on his staff.

HUNTERS

(Plates 22 and 35)

Tribal hunters are generally clad in a costume made of leaves. They wear a small cap similar to a coronet in shape, also fashioned from foliage (Phase I, south face, west part, 3.3). Invariably they are armed with bow and arrows. Among the recurrent characters is the hunter carrying a dead animal across his shoulder; the huntress leaning on her bow (Phase I, south face, west part, 3.3 and South Staircase, south face 1.2 and east face 1.1), and the hunter extracting a thorn from the foot of the huntress. These last mentioned figures are related to the myth of Narasimha's sojourn among the Chenchus[12] and the trials he had to undergo before obtaining the hand of Chenchu-Lakshmi.

FEMALE DANCERS

(Plates 42 and 83)

The costume of the kolata-dancers remains unaltered from the 14th to the early 16th centuries. It consists of a pleated skirt, but it is not clear whether the dancers wear a bodice. Dancers have their long hair tied into large buns resting on the nape of their necks, or more commonly gathered into plaits. They wear all the usual jewellery: necklaces of various designs, large round earrings, bracelets, and anklets.

In the 16th century short skirts, barely knee-length, came into fashion for both kolata-dancers and classical dancers. Close fitting tights are seen beneath the short pleated skirts, which may be two or three-tiered, and occasionally have fringe-like trimmings (Phase IV, bottom series, upper gala, north part, 8). An array of elaborate girdles of various designs completes this glamorous attire. The simplest type of waistband consists of a sash ending in an elegant pleated fan at the front; there are, however, different ways of tying it, so as to achieve a two- or three-tiered effect. Another type of waist ornament consists of three decorative loops of decreasing length hanging from the girdle. The longest of these ornaments reaches the knees; other examples are proportionately shorter (Phase IV, bottom series, upper gala, north part, 9). The hair is tied into a large bun, either pinned on the crown of the head at a slight angle or positioned to the side of the head. The dancers wear an impressive array of jewellery, such as necklaces of various lengths, massive earrings, armlets, bracelets and anklets (Phase IV, middle series, gala, south part, 8).

OTHER WOMEN

(Plate 82)

The female attire is rather simple, consisting as it does of a lower garment pleated at the front, an elaborate sash and the occasional long scarf hanging around the shoulder in an elegant loop at the back. The hair is tied in a bun, sometimes at the side of the head (Phase II, south face, 3.36) and they wear the usual jewellery.

In Phases I, II and III there are few representations of women other than the dancers on the east and south faces of the South Staircase. However, in Phase IV there are a number of female courtly attendants which are prominently depicted. They belong to the entourage of kings and noblemen, and often carry a sword, a pouch for betel leaves, and a chauri (Phase IV, bottom series, upper gala, north part, 9). These attendants wear a long piece of material tied below the waist, but it is difficult to establish whether this garment is tied like a dhoti or a lungi; often it has an elegant pleated fan at the front. The girdle worn above the lower garment is constituted by various decorative strings, as in the case of the dancers; otherwise it looks like a pleated sash, or it imitates the bead-festoon motif similar to that carved on to the pillars. The hairstyles are more diverse than those seen in the other phases. The bun is placed either on the side or on the crown of the head. Occasionally, however, the bun on the nape of the neck and the plait are still seen, but they are apparently no longer the fashion of the day. Head ornaments are conspicuously shown, especially pins, studs, chains and fillets that enhance carefully rendered, elaborate coiffures.

ANIMALS AND BIRDS

(Plates 7, 14, 17, 20, 23, 25, 32, 38, 43, 44, 46, 55, 56, 58 to 60, 62 and 80)

The most spectacular examples of animal depictions occur in Phases I and II. Numerous hunting scenes bear testimony to the keen observation of nature on the part of the artists. Gazelles, bears, boars, tigers, lions, dogs and monkeys have been rendered with immediacy and empathy. Running, jumping, climbing on trees, mating, fighting, or fleeing before dogs and hunters, these animals have pride of place, especially the hunting scenes on Phase I, while human figures are often only accessories to the scenes. The freshness of approach and lively treatment of the subject are of outstanding artistic interest.

The most frequently depicted animals are gazelles. Their elegant movement are evidently a source of great inspiration for the artists, who delighted in depicting them jumping, grazing, scratching their noses against the hind leg, mating, and fighting with horns interlocked (Phase I, south face, west part, 3.1). In some instances the composition is determined by the movement of a jumping gazelle filling the block diagonally: the animal is attacked by dogs (Phase I, south face, west part, 3.11), or jumps in a forested landscape suggested by a tree (Phase II, south face, 3.35). Occasionally gazelles are shown with double heads: one grazing, the other raised in alert towards the approaching hunter (Phase II, east face, south part, 4.92). Groups of gazelles have been differently rendered: sometimes their bodies almost totally overlapping, as in the three jumping animals with their heads pointing in different directions (Phase I, south face, west part, 3.1), in clusters (Phase I, south face, west part, 3.10), or attacked by dogs (Phase I, south face, west part, 3.11).

Dogs are shown on the leash or chasing the prey. A particularly vivid rendering of a dog on the leash is carved on the South Staircase (south face, 1.1). Here, a hunter barely manages to restrain a large dog eager to pounce on its prey. A less dramatic scene is shown in Phase I, where a beater is accompanied by two dogs, one of which is on the leash (south face, west part, 3.6). A large number of hunting scenes shows dogs chasing animals, attacking them, and once they have been wounded, pouncing on them, as in the boar hunt on the South Staircase (south face, 1.3 and east face,1.1).

Tigers on the prowl are another popular theme. On Phase I (south face, west part, 2.6 and 3.12) and the South Staircase (south face, 1.1) tigers are stabbed by hunters; in another scene a hunter and his retainer have to flee to a tree top before the raging tiger is killed (Phase I, south face, west part 3.7). More uncertain is the outcome between a man and a tiger elsewhere on Phase I; the man in his helpless situation raises the hands in a gesture of despair (north face, west part, 3.2). Another dramatic scene is found on Phase II, in which a hunter is besieged by tigers climbing on the tree on which he sought refuge (south face, 3.7, 3.8 and 4.15). More unconventional themes are also seen on this phase of the monument. In one example, two bulls or buffaloes are confronted by a tiger (west face, south part, 4.1); in another, a tiger is charged by an enraged bull (west face, north part, 6.99). Sometimes tigers are shown resting in a sylvan landscape (Phase II, west face south part, 4.13) or pacing beneath a tree (west face, south part, 4.11).

Bears and boars appear prominently in the narratives of Narasimha's adventures among the Chenchus on the South Staircase (bottom rows). The scene in which a huge boar pierced by an arrow rises up on his hind legs and is then attacked by dogs is particularly striking (south face, 1.3). Elsewhere, a bear rears menacingly on its hind legs (South Staircase, east face, 1.2). Here the artist decided to devote the whole block to the depiction of the animal.

Monkeys are also found in the carvings on Phase II. On the south face (2.17) is a visual pun consisting of four monkeys, two facing opposite directions, connected to each other by two additional bodies. This theme is further explored on the west face where the majority of carvings depicts monkeys climbing or perching on trees (west face, south part, 3.3 and 3.5). An unusual composition (3.4) shows a huge monkey surrounded by smaller ones sitting beneath a tree. Monkeys eat fruit beneath a tree (south face, 4.39 and west face, north part, 6.100); elsewhere a monkey seated opposite a tree holds a snake in its hands (south face, 4.32). It is not clear whether the last mentioned scene is inspired by a popular story of the time. A more traditional theme appears in Phase I, where a monkey tries to disrobe a woman (west face, south part, 4.3).

Camels appear frequently in the carvings on Phases I and II. Impressive are the rendering of caravans (Phase I, south face, 5.2 and 5.4 and west face, south part, 5.1). These scenes are generally headed by a groom leading a camel on which a kettledrum-player is seated. The theme of the camel and kettledrum-player appears also on its own (first and last scene on the top row of the rear wall of the East Entrance Chamber). These are the sole depiction of camels in Phase III.

Apart from the unusual carvings in which bulls or buffaloes confront tigers (Phase II, west face, south part, 4.1 and west face, north part, 6.99), there is also a depiction of a bull mounted by a diminutive, Central Asian figure of a kettle-drum player (Phase I, west face, south part, 5.1).

Depictions of elephants and horses are ubiquitous, as in the procession of elephants uprooting trees on Phase I (south face, west part, 6th row). The theme of the elephant at work is repeated at various places on the South Staircase (east and south faces, top rows, as well as on the balustrade). It also occurs on Phases III (south face, 2.1) and IV (bottom series, jagati and middle series, lower upana). Both these courses are almost exclusively devoted to elephants walking, uprooting shrubs or trees, and occasionally getting out of control. Enraged elephants occur at various places. One of the most dramatic depictions is that carved on Phases II (west face, north part, 6.97 and north face, west part, 6.2) and IV (middle series, lower upana, south part, 15 and north part, 10 and 11). Elephants confronting tigers appear in Phase I, South face, 6.4, in which a growling tiger approaches stealthily an elephant, and in Phase IV (bottom series, lower gala, north part, 6). In this last depiction, a tiger leaps on the trunk of an elephant. An unusual carving in Phase II (south face, 3.34) shows an elephant carrying a tiger on its back; similarly, in the East Entrance Chamber a monkey (?) rides on an elephant (rear wall, third row).

Horses are as popular as elephants, and they appear on all phases. Especially noteworthy are the depictions of the 'state horse', richly caparisoned and shaded by an umbrella, which occur only on Phase II (e.g. south face, 3.11, 4.38 and 4.40) Otherwise, horses are paraded by foreign traders and grooms (e.g. Phase I, south face, west part, 4.12, and west face, north part, 3.100, and East Entrance Chamber, south wall), or ridden by both local and foreign troops (Phase I, south face, west part, 2.2 and west face, south part, 4.1). Horses also appear progressing in long processional friezes (Phase IV, bottom series, lower gala, north part) Unidentified animals appear repeatedly (Phase I, west face, north part, 2.100) as well as in the complex hunting scenes on Phase I (south face, west part, 3rd row), in which weathering and flaking prevent their precise identification.

Fabulous animals such as the gajavrishabha appear in Phases I (south face, west part, 6.9, (fragment) and II (south face, 4.14). A mythical animal with a lion's body and an elephant's head is also found (Phase I, south face, west part, 6.11, and South Staircase balustrade). Among these imaginary creatures the makara has pride of place, as on the South Staircase. The creeper running continuously all along both faces (rows 2 and 6) issues from the mouth of a makara concealed among the rhyzomes, among which the hamsas are carved. On the balustrade, the shrub which the elephant uproots issues from the mouth of a makara carved in shallow relief on the left.

Birds also have great role to play. Foremost are the hamsas, which appear in gracefully meandering friezes of creepers on the South Staircase (east and south faces, 2nd and 6th rows, as well as Phase II, south face, 6.1 to 6.6). The hamsa/mayuras are interspersed among the decorative and architectural motifs of Phase III (gala). The classic motif of the hamsa in foliage medallion adorns the walls of the staircases leading upwards from the East Entrance Chamber. The carvings here consist exclusively of hamsas, ducks and peacocks.

Other varieties of birds are also appear in the sculptures. In Phase II there is a rather unusual series of birds, including peacocks, water birds and storks (west face, south part, row 2 and west face, north part, row 5). Some of these are depicted in their natural surroundings, on a background of leaves or flowers (west face, south part, 2.7); others are treated as heraldic symbols, as for instance the pair of peacocks with intertwined necks (west face, north part, 5.92). Finally, a parrot is shown perching on the hand of a woman (south face, 3.36).

Series of birds, mainly peacocks, are carved on Phase II (south face, 6.7 and 6.9), as well as on the blocks of the eastern extension (Phase I, south face, east part, 4.3, 4.4, 4.5, 7.1 and 7.2).

TREES, SHRUBS AND CREEPERS

A wide variety of trees is depicted on Phases I and II. Artists were keen observer of natural surroundings, taking pride in illustrating the various species. One of the most striking examples is the 'flowering' tree with a peacock strutting beneath (Phase I, south face, west part, 2.4). Here the crown of the tree is inhabited by a small feline. The same tree also appears elsewhere (Phase I, south face, west part, 2.6 and east part, 7.7), but does not appear in later phases. Other trees appear in Phase I, such as the tall tree on the South Staircase (east and south faces, 7.1), the crown of which is occasionally inhabited by a pair of parrots, shown back to back, but twisting their heads so as to face each other. A squirrel (or chipmunk) scuttles on the trunk of one of these trees (South Staircase east face, 7.1), while elephants either uproot shrubs growing beneath, or plunge their trunk into their lush crowns. Trees appear regularly in the many depictions of elephants at work, as in the last example. Elephants are also chained to the trunk of a tree (Phase IV, middle series, lower upana, south part, 12). Trees are used to define the various phases of the action in a narrative as exemplified in the rendering of the adventures of Narasimha among the Chenchus on the South Staircase (east and south faces, 1), or in the numerous hunting scenes (especially Phase II, east face, south part, 4.91 and 4.92), as well as in processional scenes, such as the caravan of camels on Phase I (south face, west part, 5.1).

Trees are not merely accessory elements; they are also occasionally the main subject of a scene, as when a tree fills the whole block (Phase II, west face, north part, 6.100 and south face, 3.15, 4.8 and 4.31). A fabulous tree inhabited by monkeys and birds is repeated on Phase II (south face, 2.6 and 4.19). The theme of a tree inhabited by monkeys is further explored in Phase II (west face, south part, 3.3 and 3.5). Finally, the crown of a tree provides shelter to hunters chased by wild animals (Phase I, south face, west part, 3.7 and Phase II, south face, 4.15).

The interest of artists in the rendering of nature diminishes abruptly with Phase II. On Phase III the rendering of natural surrounding is limited to the background of the scenes carved on the rear wall of the East Entrance Chamber (row 3). Trees and shrubs on Phase IV are rendered in a formulaic manner, which bears no resemblance to the keen depictions of the previous Phases. Stylized shrubs appear on all phases, generally along with elephants. Occasionally, shrubs and bushes are used as divisional device between scenes (Phase I, south face, west part, 3.3).

NOTES

1. See the portraits of Mallikarjuna and his chauri-bearer Shirangu carved either side of the

entrance to the sanctuary of the so-called Anjaneya temple (Verghese 1991: 51-2).

2. According to Domingo Paes such a scarf was given as a 'token of friendship and love' (Sewell, 1970 [1900]: 244).
3. Verghese (1991: 52). Wagoner (1995: 8-9) writes: 'It is noteworthy that both kabayi (tunic) and kullayi are new to South India in the Vijayanagara period; in fact their adoption represents a radical departure from earlier traditions of Indic courtly dress. Prior to the kabayi in the fourteenth or early fifteenth century, men at South India courts did not customarily wear any upper garment, but instead left their chests and arms exposed, or at most, loosely draped their shoulders with a long, rectangular piece of untailored cloth. Similarly, before the introduction of the kullayi, pre-formed hats or caps of fabric were unheard of in South India, where rulers typically wore a jeweled crown (kirita or karanda makuta) or narrow fillet (patta). Despite their novelty, however, the kabayi and kullayi were not new inventions of the Vijayanagara period; to the contrary, the evidence overwhelmingly indicates that they appeared as adaptations of items in common use throughout the Islamic world. This is suggested both by their names, clearly loanwords from the Arabic and Persian qaba and kulah, and by their close correspondence with the Islamic garments designated by these two terms.'
4. Duarte Barbosa, quoted in Verghese (1991: 56).
5. See, *Mohana Tarangini* (*c.* 1550), XLI, 57. Noblemen wore following ornaments: 'Golden headgear, studded with gems; ear ornaments, shoulder ornaments, armlets, various types of necklaces of pearls, beads and precious stones, bracelets, finger rings.' Translation by C.T.M. Kotraiah (unpublished).
6. *Mohana Tarangini*, XXII, 4-46.
7. *Bharatesha Vaibhava Sangraha* (1457), XVI, 1-6.
8. Verghese (1991: 56). Duarte Barbosa and Cesare Federici both refer to shoes in their travelogues; see Filliozat (1999: 302-4 and 328).
9. An extensive description of the various military contingents is to be found in the *Ramanatha Charite*, *c.* 1525. Although this is a relatively late text, some of the costumes and weapons described are very similar to those depicted in the sculptures: 'Then there were the lancers. They held short daggers, wore tight lower garments with hanging tassels. They had big hair buns and had applied sandal paste over their bodies. Next came the bodyguards; they were dressed in tight shorts, gold ornaments, silk (turbans) and anklets. They also carried glittering swords and new shields . . . and a new kind of sword, called kadi-tale (chop the head off)', XI, 36-38. See Kotraiah and Dallapiccola (2003: 69).
10. Sewell (1970 [1900]: 265).
11. Goetz (1966: 66-70).
12. The Chenchus live in the Nallamalai range, a forested area to the south of the Krishna River and the Srisailam plateau. Literary and artistic traditions represent them wearing clothes and headdresses of leaves. They were reputedly very good hunters, and expert forest guides. They style themselves 'brothers-in-law of Narasimha', (of Ahobilam) which they call Obalesudu. According to the traditional story Narasimha, while wandering through the forests, met a lovely Chenchu girl and wanted to marry her. Her father, however, a Chenchu chieftain, put the suitor through a series of tests, such as climbing tall trees, digging termite hills, hunting fierce beasts, collecting wild honey. Finally, having proved himself, he married the girl, who became known as Chenchu-Lakshmi (Verghese 1995: 39). The connection of the Vijayanagara Rayas with the Ahobilam temples dates back to the period of Harihara II (1377-1404) (Sitapati 1982: 14).

Chapter Six

CARVINGS OF PHASE I

SOUTH FACE, EAST PART

1.6 This panel, almost completely buried, shows a forest scene filled with various animals and trees.

2.1 A groom, a staff in his hands, restrains three elephants. His hair is tied in a bun resting on the nape of the neck. Due to the weathered state of the panel, the details of the costume are difficult to make out. He probably wears a knee-length, lower garment and is bare-chested. Traces of trappings are to be discerned on the elephants. The animals, of different sizes, proceed towards the left. The groom faces towards the right.

2.2 Three soldiers, armed with curved swords and small round shields move from left to right. Their attire consists of a knee-length, lower garment, with a long sash falling in decorative folds tied at the front. On their heads they wear what seem to be a helmet (?). A tree on the right concludes the block.

2.3 Seven soldiers attired as in 2.2, proceed through a forested landscape, suggested by a tree placed between the last man to the left, and the remaining six men. What makes this group interesting is the concern of the artist to introduce a variety of movements in the figures. This is achieved in a simple, yet ingenious way: while the men proceed from left to right, their heads are oriented variously: the first man from the right faces the viewer; the second man looks towards the left; the third and the fourth men look at each other, one brandishing his sword high above his head, the other resting it on the right shoulder; the fifth man looks over his shoulder; the sixth man looks over his shoulder at the last man near the tree. Together with the figures shown on 2.2 and 2.3 they probably formed a linked sequence.

2.4 Two hunting scenes. On the right part a right-facing hunter aims an arrow at a cluster of animals depicted as if standing on top of each other; a boar (?) at the bottom, tiger in the middle and gazelle on top. The foreground is enlivened by two birds. On the left part are two hunters, both facing to the left. The first hunter, in the middle of the panel, shoots an arrow at a jumping gazelle. A dog is near to him. The second hunter carries bow and arrow in his hands. The two scenes can be interpreted as self-contained units. However, it is possible that these scenes belonged to longer narrative, together with 2.5 and 2.6.

2.5 Three hunting scenes. From the right, the first tableau depicts a right-facing hunter who is concealed behind a tree, aiming arrows at a group of animals in a forest clearing. Three gazelles are attacked by the hunter's dog, while a tiger prowls at a distance. The feet of the tiger rest on a small shelf, a device seen occasionally in other carvings of Phase I. The climactic central scene depicts a leaping tiger attacked by two dogs. The animal proceeding from the right is faced by a hunter who aims an arrow at it. The man's exertion is expressed in the dramatic twist of his body: legs oriented towards the left; head and chest facing to the right. A tree separates this scene from the next, in which a right-facing hunter shoots an arrow at a jumping gazelle. *(Plates 7 and 8)*

2.6 The last block of this row is occupied by a beater carrying a stick in his right hand, and holding a dog on the leash with his left hand.

The right-facing man walks towards 2.5. The figures in this hunting sequence wear a short lower garment enlivened at the front by a sash. Some wear necklaces; all have their hair tied in buns resting on the napes of the necks. *(Plate 8)*

3.1 This small and weathered block is devoted exclusively to animals. Among these are three antelopes, two of which are shown copulating.

3.2 Four forest scenes. In the first scene, a hunter carrying a bow in the right hand and an arrow in the raised left hand walks through a forest teeming with animals. In the background is the deer (?) he has just shot; in the foreground a group of gazelles. One gazelle, standing on its hind legs on the verge of jumping away, stares backwards. Another gazelle is shown grazing; it lifts its head towards the approaching hunter. The weathered state of the panel does not allow one to identify the other animals, except for a boar, more gazelles and some smaller game. A tree separates the first scene from the second, in the middle of which is a tiger (?) surrounded by animals. A second tree introduces the third scene, in which a dog stands over a gazelle lying dead on the ground. The background is enlivened by a bear (?), while the foreground has a leaping antelope. An unidentified figure is carved beneath the tree that separates this scene from the fourth and last scene. Here, a boar and other animals peacefully graze in a forest dale.

3.3 to **3.11** Infill blocks.

3.12 Three camels move towards the left, where a decoratively rendered tree concludes the block. *(Plates 6 and 7)*

3.13 A soldier with a curved sword resting on his left shoulder and round shield in his right hand moves towards the left. His attire, which cannot be clearly studied because of the poor condition of the carving, maybe similar to that of the soldiers in 2.2 and 2.3. *(Plate 6)*

4.1 A horseman with raised right announces the arrival of a nobleman. The nobleman rides on a rearing horse and is followed by a retainer and a parasol-bearer, both on foot. The group is preceded by two Central Asian grooms, wearing long cloaks, each in charge of a horse. Due to weathering most of the finer details of the costumes have disappeared.

4.2 A Central Asian trader wearing conspicuously rendered boots parades two horses. This carving is probably part of 4.1.

4.3, 4.4 and **4.5** Three blocks showing various birds. Three birds are depicted in 4.3: an unidentifiable first bird pecks at its foot; a second bird looks like a dove; a third bird is a peacock. Two peacocks are carved on 4.4, and three peacocks on 4.5.

4.6 to **4.11** Infill blocks.

4.12 This has a crudely hewn, female figure. The lady, with a strikingly big head on a diminutive body, carries a pet bird on her wrist. *(Plate 6)*

5.2 Partially sculpted. To the right, a groom restrains a prancing horse. An elegant tree enlivens the background. A tree and a horse are barely visible in the roughly hewn left-hand part of the block.

6.1 Three elephants pace towards the left. A tree delimits the block to the right.

6.2 This weathered block is the continuation of 6.1. All that remains is the rendering of an elephant heading to the left. There are faint traces of a second pacing elephant.

7.1 Two birds; the first one, to the right, pecks something off the ground.

7.2 Seven birds in a forested landscape. The first bird from the right is shown pecking at something on the ground; the second bird, separated from the first by a tree, is depicted with two heads, one inspecting the ground, the other looking back towards the right. Another tree separates the second and third birds. The latter greedily plunges its beak into what seems to be a tree (or a huge flower?). The remaining four birds, of different sizes, peck at the ground.

7.7 Two decorative trees and the hind parts of an elephant pacing towards the left.

8.1 Six birds, possibly peacocks, in a landscape. The layout of the carvings follows the scheme of 7.2. The birds are separated from each other by foliage motifs. In order to impart movement to the composition the head of the birds are differently oriented. The first bird looks towards the left; the second bird pecks in the ground; the head of the third bird faces to the right; the heads of the fourth and the fifth birds face to the left; the sixth bird is barely visible.

SOUTH FACE, WEST PART

Parades and Scenes of Courtly Life

2.1 Blocked by the stairs.

2.2 From right to left: The central figure of this scene is a nobleman riding a richly caparisoned horse. His uplifted arm points towards the left. He is followed by a parasol-bearing retainer on foot and two horse riding attendants. He is preceded by a sword-bearer and three large armed men. Their attire consists of short lower garments with sashes falling in decorative folds tied at the front, and helmets (?) (see also east part of 2.2). They carry curved swords and small round shields. As elsewhere on Phase I, these soldiers are shown taller and sturdier than footmen; it is probable that they belonged to some special corps. Although moving towards the left, they look back towards the group of mounted noblemen on the right. Footmen dressed in short lower garments with their hair tied in buns, carrying swords (or spears), concludes the scene to the left. In order to suggest a crowd these figure are arranged in a 'fish-scale' formation, with one figure partly overlapping the other. Their heads, however, are variously oriented to the right or left. *(Plate 10)*

2.3 The right end of this block is occupied by four retainers of the nobleman in 2.2, marching to the left. A tree separates this rather formal procession from a sequence of two hunting scenes. From right to left: In the first scene, a tiger stalks a hunter concealed in the branches of a tree. Following the conventions of the continuous narration, the tiger appears a second time leaping towards him. The man, holding a bow in his left hand, plunges the dagger into the throat of the animal with his right hand, while his dog at the foot of the tree jumps towards the tiger, furiously barking. In the background three gazelles flee, thereby adding to the drama. A calmer mood pervades the second scene. A hunter armed with bow and arrow walks towards the forest in the company of a retainer and two dogs. This sequence could equally be read from left to right. The theme of the hunter concealing from wild animals in the crown of a tree appears also on 3.7, as well as elsewhere on Phase II (south face, 3.7, 3.8 and 4.15).

2.4 Two different themes are illustrated here. The right-hand part accommodates a spirited dance and music performance by two Central Asian dancers flanked by two tambourine-players. In spite of the weathered condition it is still possible to recognize the knee-length tunics of the men, their ribbed conical caps with upturned brims and their long billowing scarves. (A more famous version of this theme is seen on 5.2.) The left-hand part of this block is occupied by a magnificent rendering of an oversized peacock, with a tendril in its beak. The bird struts majestically before a diminutive, yet decorative flowering tree inhabited by a feline (?).

2.5 The left-hand part shows three courtly figures comfortably seated on a platform, the base of which has carved birds, flowers (?) and a tiger and boar (?) facing one another. The trio of figures is shown intently watching a boxing match that occupies the right-hand part. The first of the three figures, probably a royal person, occupies the centre of the composition. He is seated with his left leg crossed over the right leg, his right elbow resting on a bolster, his left hand gracefully raised. His jewellery, yajnopavita as well as general attire and hairstyle are painstakingly rendered. Behind him, on the platform, stands a small chauri-bearer. The two other men are portrayed in a less formal manner. They are seated with their legs crossed, their right hands raised as if commenting on the boxers' performance. Two oversized athletes face one another, ready to strike. They are dressed in short lower garments, their hair is probably concealed by caps, or possibly closely cropped; their closed fists seem to be bare. Between the seated group and the boxers stands a dignified figure with his hands resting on a staff, also following the match with rapt attention. This could be one of the members of the royal household, perhaps a 'master of ceremonies'. *(Plates 26 and 27)*

2.6 A sequence of three forest scenes. From right to left: The first scene shows a tiger leaping on a man, who kills the rearing animal by thrusting his dagger into its mouth (see 2.3). The carving is impressive for its vigour and immediacy. A superb flowering tree, similar to the one in 2.4, introduces the second scene, which depicts a forest glade teeming with animals. Two boars graze in the foreground, while three gazelles jump in the background. A second tree marks the transition to the next phase of action, at the left hand of the block. Concealed behind its trunk a hunter, accompanied by a retainer armed with a long spear, aims at the animals in the clearing. This sequence of scenes may also be read form left to right. *(Plate 19)*

2.7 The last three blocks of this row depict a long military parade proceeding from right to left. The parade starts with three horsemen, of which the first from the left is possibly a foreigner. All three figures flourish their swords. The trio is preceded by a group of seven footmen carrying spears, the upper ends of which protrude into the row above. The men wear the usual short lower garments, with long sashes draped in pleats at the front; their hair tied in buns. *(Plates 11 and 13)*

2.8 Two soldiers armed with curved swords and small round shields, dressed as in 2.2, follow a man riding on a horse brandishing a sword in his left hand. The latter is preceded by one additional soldier. The block ends with the rendering of two horsemen: that on the left curbs his rearing horse with a whip (?). *(Plate 11)*

2.9 Two horsemen; the first from the right wears a helmet. They are preceded by a retinue of seven footmen armed with long spears. As noted in 2.7, the upper portions of the weapons protrude into the blocks above. The footmen arrive at the presence of a seated royal figure, his left leg crossed over his right leg, leaning comfortably on a bolster. The details of dress and ornament are particularly clear: a thin band encircles his head, keeping the heavy bun at the nape of the neck in place; the necklaces, armlets, bracelets and knee-length lower garment are carefully rendered. A male chauri-bearer stands in attendance behind. The courtly personage is shown conversing with two foreigners dressed in flowing robes, the sleeves of which cover their hands. On their heads they wear caps with long streamers. *(Plates 29 to 31)*

Hunting

3.1 From left to right: A nobleman and his diminutive attendant on a hunting spree. The man with conspicuous beard and moustache is clad in a short lower garment pleated at the front, relieved by decorative chains. A pleated sash, in which a dagger is stuck, completes the attire. Necklaces, bracelets, armlets and earrings are all painstakingly rendered. A narrow band tied around the head keeps the hair and bun in place. The rest of the panel accommodates an inventive and complex depiction of animal life. The hunter aims at his prey from behind a perfunctorily rendered tree, on which perch two parrots. The birds are shown back to back, preening their feathers. (The same theme is found on the South Staircase, east face, 7.1, and south face, 7.1.) The immediate targets of the hunter are gazelles fleeing in terror from his dog. Three further gazelles jump away in the distance. Eventually two animals are shot, and the dog sniffs (or nibbles) one of them. Further to the right a tiger pounces on a gazelle. Partly obscured by the abutting steps, the hunter's attendant stabs the hind parts of a boar (?) with a dagger. Subsidiary scenes cluster around the main episode: in the foreground are fighting animals; in the background a gazelle grazes, while two males fight near it, interlocking their horns; another gazelle scratches its nose with its hind hoof while other animals pace nearby. *(Plate 20)*

3.2 Two male figures conversing. They sit on a high throne or platform, the mouldings of which are carefully rendered.

3.3 In the left-hand part a hunter armed with bow and arrow is accompanied by an attendant, possibly a beater, carrying a stick. In order to suggest the forest environment, the artist has sculpted a diminutive gazelle fleeing 'out of the block', behind the beater. In the right-hand part, separated from latter by a shallow-carved tree inhabited by a bird, a tribal hunter, dressed in a leaf skirt and a cap made of foliage, carries a dead animal on his shoulders. Nearby, a huntress, also in leafy garments, leans gracefully against the bow that she holds in her left hand. A palm-like tree completes the panel. (The rendering of this hunting couple is similar to Narasimha and Chenchu-Lakshmi on the South Staircase, south face, 1.2, and east face, 1.1.) *(Plate 22)*

3.4 A hunter dressed in a short lower garment aims his arrows at a group of three jumping gazelles, decoratively arranged in a circle. The only prominent feature of his costume is the dagger stuck into the waistband. A tree concludes the block to the left.

3.5 Forest scene. Two hunters armed with bows and arrows, aim at the numerous animals in the middle of the composition. The hunter on the right is partly concealed by a tree, on which are perched two parrots shown back to back. The hunter on the left has come into the open, leaving behind him a tree teeming with birds and monkeys. Both figures are accompanied by dogs. Two gazelles lie wounded on the ground, while the other gazelles flee from the dog that attacks them. The hunter proceeding from the left has hit one animal, which is depicted in the act of falling to the ground (top of the block). In the foreground his dog attacks a boar; animals nearby graze peacefully. A tiger leaps on a gazelle in the background.

3.6 A bearded beater carrying a flat stick walks towards the left. He is accompanied by two dogs, one on a leash. *(Plates 24 and 25)*

3.7 Three scenes are found here. From the left: a hunter, accompanied by a beater with a stick resting on his right shoulder and an attendant with a dog on a leash, aims his arrows at a group of four gazelles jumping towards a thicket, the trees and bushes of which are decoratively rendered in shallow relief. The second scene shows the hunter shooting arrows at jumping gazelles, while his attendant thrusts his huge spear in the stomach of a rearing tiger. A boar, at the foot of a large tree growing near a cross-shaped tank, watches unperturbed. In the third scene of this dramatic hunting expedition a hunter and attendant are concealed in the crown of the tree in the preceding scene. While an attendant repels the attack of a rearing tiger by thrusting his dagger into its mouth, the hunter perched on a branch, showers arrows on a herd of grazing gazelles. *(Plate 24)*

3.8 A hunter, with bow in the left hand and arrow in the right hand, strides purposefully towards the right.

3.9 A beater walks towards the left accompanied by a dog. The man carries a stick in his right hand and an unidentified object in his left hand.

3.10 From left to right: The block is divided into two portions: the left-hand portion is occupied by a cluster of animals, possibly gazelles, and two dogs. One dog sits; the other leaps behind a hunter who occupies the centre of the composition, connecting the two phases of the action. In the right-hand portion the hunter aims his arrows towards a deer and two gazelles, one of which has been caught by one of the dogs. A boar grazes in the foreground.

3.11 Two dogs attack a jumping gazelle. One of the dogs, coming from the right, bites the hind legs of the gazelle. To the left, a second dog, rearing on its hind legs, is on the verge of jumping on the gazelle's rump. *(Plate 23)*

3.12 From right to left, three scenes. In the first scene a hunter aims his arrows 'out of the block', probably at the gazelle in 3.11. The second scene shows a beater with a flat stick resting on his right shoulder and a dog on a leash walking towards a tree. In the third scene a hunter thrusts his dagger into the throat of a rearing tiger. The three figures wear the usual knee-length, lower garments, enlivened by elegantly draped, long sashes; their long hair is tied in buns resting on the napes of their necks. *(Plate 23)*

3.13 The first scene on this block shows a cluster of animals, some are grazing while others, such as gazelles and wild asses, jump towards the left. In the next scenes the direction of movement shifts towards the right. The second scene portrays a hunter who has just shot an arrow at a gazelle, piercing its neck. A group of terrified animals jumps away, helter skelter, in the background; other animals graze unperturbed in the foreground. In the third scene, a beater, brandishing the characteristic stick, holds a dog on a leash, while his other dog, unleashed, has caught a fleeing gazelle by its hind leg. In the background are two unidentified animals and a peacock.

3.14 Two men armed with bows and arrows walk towards the right. They are followed by a woman carrying a flower, or possibly an arrow.

Horses and Grooms

4.1 From right to left: The first scene shows a groom with a horse; unfortunately the figure is damaged. The next scene depicts a Central Asian horseman on a prancing charger, brandishing a sword in his right hand. He wears a cap with upturned brim and his hair is gathered in a pigtail(?). He is preceded by a running footman carrying a parasol. While running, the footman turns his head back in the direction of the horseman. The brisk movement of the central scene contrasts effectively with the overall formal tone of the composition. The last scene depicts a horse led by a foreign groom. The man is attired in trousers and jacket; he wears a pleated turban.

4.2 From right to left: This portrays to horsemen, one cantering, the other pacing. Both figures carry unsheathed swords in their right hands, pointing towards the left. The details of the saddles, cloths and bridles are painstakingly rendered. *(Plates 15 and 21)*

4.3 From right to left: Two soldiers armed with round shields and curved swords march towards the left. Their heads, however, face to the right, which is the direction from which the two horsemen on 4.2 arrive. The central scene has two horses, one prancing, the other pacing, together with grooms. The men, one tall and lanky, the other short and sturdy, wear short loincloths. The figure at the left-hand end of the block is a foreigner on a prancing horse, pointing with his sword to the left. The focus of the composition is, however, the horses and their grooms. *(Plates 12 and 17)*

4.4 From right to left: Three pacing horses and their grooms. Due to the bad state of preservation the details of the horses' trappings and grooms' attires have been obliterated. The group proceeds at a pace in a dignified manner.

4.5 A left-facing local groom holds the bridle of the horse in 4.6.

4.6 A left-facing horse. It is possible that 4.4 to 4.6 form a continuous narrative sequence.

4.7 From right to left: The right-hand portion of the block shows a nobleman riding a rearing horse, followed by two retainers on foot. One retainer carries a parasol; the other wears a conspicuous shawl on the left shoulder. At the centre of the block, linking the two action filled scenes, is a standing figure carrying a long stick. His long cloak and cap with streamers (?) identify him as Central Asian. The action is resumed in the left-hand portion of the block, where a local rider proudly brandishes a sword and a groom pulls a reluctant horse by the bridle. *(Plate 16)*

4.8 From right to left: A rider wearing what appears to be a helmet flourishes a sword in his raised right hand.

4.9 From right to left: A Central Asian rider with the typical cap proceeds towards the west. It is not clear whether he carries a sword in his raised hand. He is preceded by three turbaned soldiers with round shields and curved swords as in 4.3. Though moving to the left, they look at the rider behind them to the right. The depiction of a local horseman concludes the block to the left.

4.10 From east to west, five horsemen. The first figure, a local man, brandishes a sword; the second figure, a Central Asian, wears a cap with upturned brim and long pigtail; the third figure, possibly also a foreigner, wears a helmet (?) and sports a triangular beard. The trio rides on prancing horses. The remaining two horsemen, one wearing a turban, the other with his long hair tied in a bun, canter towards the left. *(Plate 14)*

4.11 Blank.

4.12 From left to right: The first figure of this block is a foreign horseman proceeding at a gallop. The remainder of the block is occupied by a groom wearing a triangular cap and a long pigtail, parading an unsaddled horse, and by two traders in flowing robes, who stand respectfully before a foreign nobleman or ruler. The nobleman, who wears a headgear and a conspicuous pigtail(?), sits cross-legged on a high throne. The depiction of a local groom leading a horse concludes the block to the left. *(Plate 18)*

Camels, Grooms and Dancers

5.1 Damaged. Camels (?).

5.2 Three scenes. In the first scene, three camels, of which only one and a fragment of another are now visible, are led by a diminutive groom wearing a typical long cloak. The second scene depicts a foreign kettledrum player sitting on a camel. The camel procession is abruptly interrupted by a male figure inserted in between the processional and dancing scenes. This figure wears trousers and a small pointed cap and a long pigtail (?); he leans on a club. The solemn mood informing the right-hand part of the block changes suddenly with the introduction of two spirited Central Asian dancers. Originally there was a third dancer, but this has almost completely disappeared. The figures perform with gusto. The right-hand dancer has a pointed beard and conspicuous moustache. He wears a ribbed, pointed cap, and is dressed in a jacket with a 'cloud-pattern' collar and holds a long scarf behind his shoulders. The second dancer, who is similarly attired, plays the tambourine. The third dancer, now barely visible, is shown in an animated pose. They all wear pointed shoes. *(Plate 28)*

5.3 Blank.

5.4 Three camels in a landscape. The first two camels proceed from right to left towards what seems to be a palm tree; the last camel paces from left to right. A second tree concludes the panel to the left.

5.5 A left-facing camel.

5.6 Probably four pacing camels. The block is defaced.

5.7 Two (?) camels progressing towards the left. Between the animals is a palm tree. The block is defaced.

5.8 The sole surviving figure of this panel is a trumpet-player at the left-hand end of the block. The right-hand end of the block was probably occupied by two lively dancers. The fragments of a mridanga-player and the legs of a dancer are all that remain.

5.9 From right to left: A tree to the right and a decoratively rendered peacock to the left serve as frame to a scene showing a long-cloaked figure, similar to the one in 4.7, with a stick resting on the left shoulder, and two camels, one of which bears a foreign kettledrum player.

5.10 This block is divided into two unequal

parts by a plain band. The right-hand portion is occupied by two Central Asian dancers dressed in typical attire, one of whom plays the tambourine. The left-hand portion shows a foreign kettledrum player riding on a camel, preceded by another camel led by an outlandish groom.

5.11 A foreign kettledrum player seated on the back of a left-facing camel.

5.12 Three camels pacing towards the left are preceded by a young man beating a drum. The first and last camels are mounted by a Central Asian rider and a kettledrum player respectively. *(Plate 14)*

5.13 Two Central Asian dancers, one of whom plays the tambourine.

5.14 From left to right: The series of Central Asian dancers extends onto this block. The first two carvings on the right show a dancer and tambourine-player. The remainder of the block is occupied by two camels, one led by a foreign groom. The group is preceded by a small band of local musicians: a drum-player, a man beating a gong and a trumpeter. It is probable that this block and 5.15 constituted a continuous sequence.

5.15 From right to left: A Central Asian groom dressed in long robes leads a camel, on which sits a kettledrum player.

Elephants and Mythical Beasts

6.1 and **6.2** Infill.

6.3 Fragment: an elephant wraps its trunk around a palm tree.

6.4 Two men on an elephant are confronted by a growling tiger. The mahout wields a conspicuous elephant hook, while the second man turns towards a groom who follows the animal, encouraging it to face the tiger by prodding its hind parts with a forked staff. The detailed rendering of the diffident stance of the elephant and the different moods of the three men is remarkable.

6.5 Three pacing elephants. This block is defaced.

6.6 and **6.7** Damaged.

6.8 Fragment at the left end of the block: an elephant trunk.

6.9 Fragments of a gajavrishabha and elephant. To the right is a tree.

6.10 The right-hand part of the block shows an elephant wrapping its trunk around a tree. This motif is repeated three times. The block concludes to the left with a pacing elephant.

6.11 From right to left: Three animals. The first is a mythical animal with a lion body and elephant head. The second is an elephant wrapping its trunk around a tree. The block concludes with a pacing elephant. *(Plate 32)*

6.12 A left-facing elephant.

6.13 From right to left: The block begins and ends with the depiction of a tree. An elephant with rider, preceded by a local groom resting a stick on his shoulder, travel through a forested landscape, suggested by a tree at the right end of the block. The block concludes with a depiction of an elephant with its trunk wrapped around a tree.

SOUTH FACE, EXTENSION 1

1.1 Three left-facing elephants.

1.2 This block partly framed: two left-facing elephants.

1.3 An elephant wrapping its trunk around a tree. The animal faces to the left.

1.4 This framed block is divided into two parts. The right-hand part accommodates a groom leading a horse. The left-hand part, divided by a narrow plain band from the former part, shows a left-facing elephant.

1.5 Partly framed block. Two elephants moving towards the left. The trunk of the one is wrapped around the tail of the other. Between them is a groom.

2.1 A left-facing horse.

2.2 Partly framed block, divided into two parts by a plain, narrow vertical band. The two portions show each a left-facing horse.

2.3 An unfinished carving of a left-facing camel.

2.4 A gazelle (?) under a tree grooms its foreleg; a horse is led by a diminutive groom.

2.5 A left-facing camel and a horse, each led by a foreign (?) groom.

5.5 Block divided into two uneven sections. The smaller section on the right shows a left-facing camel. Two camels led by a foreign groom occupy the left-hand section.

5.6 Block divided into two sections. An elephant moving towards the left occupies the right-hand section; in the left-hand section an elephant wraps its trunk around a tree.

6.8 Two left-facing elephants.

7.4 Left-facing elephant.

8.5 Misplaced block: elephant facing the sky.

8.6 An elephant uprooting a tree. The animal faces to the left.

SOUTH FACE, EXTENSION 2

1.1 Partly obscured: hunting scene. Only the heads of three gazelles, one of which is shown dying, only the crowns of two trees are discernible.

1.2 A hunter concealed behind a tree aims his arrows at a heard of gazelles grazing in a clearing. Behind a second tree, a tiger leaps on some gazelles.

1.3 A hunter standing between two trees shoots an arrow, wounding a gazelle in the head, while another gazelle jumps away. The right-hand part of the block has a tree and two leaping gazelles.

1.4 A tree to the left of the block introduces the scene. A hunter armed with a long spear kills an unidentified animal. A similar animal concludes the scene to the right.

1.5 A hunter aims an arrow at a group of gazelles grazing in a clearing with diminutive trees. In the foreground is a boar.

1.6 Defaced.

4.1 A left-facing camel.

8.5 A left-facing elephant.

8.7 Three horses, the second of which is led by a groom, proceed towards the left.

WEST FACE, SOUTH PART

2.1 Blank.

2.2 Partly buried. Two Central Asian dancers flanked by tambourine two players. The other figures, probably also dancers and musicians, are now obscured.

2.3 Almost completely buried. Only a Central Asian hat and part of another unidentifiable figure are visible.

Hunting

3.1 Three hunting scenes. From right to left: A hunter, facing left, shoots arrows at a group of animals, mainly gazelles, one of which is captured by his dog. The animals flee towards the left, and clash with another group of gazelles, which escape towards to the right, pursued by a second hunter coming from left. The latter's dog has caught one of the animals. In the last scene, at the left end of the block, a man kills a tiger rearing on its hind paws by plunging his dagger into its gaping mouth.

3.2 Sequence of three hunting scenes. The right-hand portion of the block accommodates two hunters: one strings his bow, while the other aims his arrows at a group of gazelles. A third hunter, coming from the opposite direction, has just shot an arrow at a leaping gazelle. In the foreground, the dogs of the two parties chase and wound some animals. The central scene depicts two hunters carrying a dead gazelle tied by its hoofs to a pole. At the extreme left end of the block, yet another hunter shoots a deluge of arrows towards a cluster of gazelles (?), while his two dogs chase the terrified animals.

3.3 From left to right: a hunter, a beater with a dog on a leash, and yet another figure armed with bow and arrows stalk a group of gazelles. An unleashed dog chases the fleeing animals.

3.4 Blank.

Horsemen

4.1 A left-facing, Central Asian horseman, wearing a cap with upturned brim, proceeds at a gallop. It is not clear what he carries in the raised hand. A narrow frame runs along the edges of the block.

4.2 On this block are four Central Asian figures. Each scene is separated from the next by a narrow plain band. From right to left: in the first scene, a rider brandishing a weapon in his raised right hand proceeds at a pace towards the left, while looking in the opposite direction. In the second scene, an archer riding a left-facing horse twists his body while aiming his arrows towards the right. In the third scene, a horseman balances on a rearing horse. In his raised right hand he probably carried a sword. In the last scene, a horseman kills a tiger by transfixing it with his long spear. A narrow frame runs along the edges of the block.

4.3 A richly attired and bejewelled woman places a flower in her bun, while a monkey tries to disrobe her by pulling at her sari. The dress and decoration of the figure are particularly well rendered. A narrow frame runs along the edges of the block.

4.4 Five vignettes are divided by a vertical plain band. From right to left: in the first scene, a horseman proceeds at a pace towards the left. A sword rests on his right shoulder, and his face is oriented towards the right. The next three scenes depict Central Asian cavalry figures. The first raises his right arm while balancing on a rearing horse. The second figure rides on a pacing horse and carries a sword in his raised right hand. The third figure, brandishing an unsheathed sword, proceeds at a gallop. The fifth and last scene depicts a soldier armed with a curved sword and round shield.

4.5 A Central Asian horseman on a rearing (?) horse. This block is weathered so that the details of the carving are no longer discernible.

4.6 From right to left: a Central Asian horseman; a groom sporting a ribbed cap with fluttering streamers leading a horse, and a galloping horseman wearing the same type of cap and a long pigtail.

Camels, Musicians and Grooms

5.1 This block depicts a processional scene in which Central Asian figures play a conspicuous role. From right to left: A camel; a bull on which rides kettledrum player; a second camel also carrying a kettledrum player proceeding towards a tree in the middle; finally a third camel, on which sits a third kettledrum player, led by a groom. A tree concludes the composition to the right. Vestiges of a narrow frame run along the edges of the block.

5.2 The processional scene continues onto this block. A majestic figure in flowing robes and a ribbed cap and a long pigtail, probably a gatekeeper or guard, leans on a staff, watching the progress of the procession of camels in 5.1. The next scene shows two camels led by Central Asian grooms. In the last scene, with a tree as a backdrop, a hunter carries a dead animal on his shoulders. This probably refers to the story of Narasimha in 5.3. Vestiges of a narrow frame run along the edges of the block. *(Plate 33)*

5.3 The mythological sequence continues: Narasimha kneels down to extracts a thorn from

Chenchu-Lakshmi's foot, while she leans on her bow. The camel procession is resumed. Two Central Asians playing kettledrums sit on camels. A tree separates this scene from the next, in which a Central Asian groom holds by the bridle two camels, one facing the other.

5.4 Two Central Asian grooms lead camels. A third groom, a local man, leads two camels. The animal to the right, but facing left, bears a kettle-drum player.

5.5 The hind parts of a camel. Fragment of a partly obscured block.

Elephants and Trees

6.1 A right-facing elephant.

6.2 Group of four elephants and four trees: the first elephant from the right proceeds towards a tree; the second elephant wraps its trunk around the stem of another tree; the third elephant walks towards yet a third tree; the fourth elephant plunges its trunk into the foliage of the last tree of this sequence. A narrow frame runs along the edges of the block.

6.3 The block is divided into two parts by a narrow, plain band. The right-hand part shows two pacing elephants. In the left-hand part, an elephant wraps its trunk around a tree, while a second elephant walks towards a tree in 6.4.

6.4 A tree begins the panel on the right. The next three scenes each show elephants: the first elephant walks towards a tree; the second elephant uproots a tree; lastly, two elephants proceed towards the left.

6.5 Tree. Fragment of a partly obscured block.

WEST FACE, NORTH PART

Forest Scenes

2.97 Hind parts of a gazelle. The block is partly obscured by Phase IV.

2.98 Two scenes carved on this block illustrate completely different themes. To the right is the a hunting expedition. From left to right: a hunter shoots his arrow at a cluster of animals, killing a gazelle, while a boar grazes in the foreground. A tree separates this scene from the next. A dog attacks a grazing gazelle, while the remaining animals leap away in terror. A tree, on which climbs a monkey, marks the transition to a lively dance scene carved on the left-hand part of the block. Here two Central Asian dancers, throwing billowing scarves above their heads and around their shoulders, are accompanied by a tambourine player.

2.99 Two forest scenes. That to the right depicts a hunter who has just shot an arrow that strikes a gazelle in the neck. A dog pursues the wounded animal. In the foreground, a second dog chases a leaping gazelle, while other gazelles flee or pace elegantly. The scene concludes to the right with a monkey climbing on a tree. Divided by a tree from the previous scene, the left-hand scene has a huge buffalo with lowered head ready to charge a growling tiger. A tree concludes the scene to the left.

2.100 An unidentified animal rests beneath a tree.

Horses and Grooms

3.98 A Central Asian groom leads a horse (partly concealed). A second horse led by an attendant follows a horseman, who proceeds at a gallop, brandishing an unsheathed sword in his right hand.

3.99 Three Central Asian (?) grooms, each parading a horse. The group is preceded by a local musician beating a small, hourglass-shaped drum.

3.100 A groom wearing a ribbed cap (or turban) parades a horse before a royal figure and courtly companion. Both men sit on a throne, the royal figure with his left leg resting on the throne and his right hanging down. His right elbow rests on a bolster; his right hand is raised. The second person is sits cross-legged nearby. A figure clad in a long cloak, with a staff resting on the right shoulder (compare with the figure on the south face, western part, 4.7) stands before the seated men. Probably there was yet another figure between a groom parading the horse and a standing chowkidar.

NORTH FACE

2.1 Obscured.

Horsemen

3.1 A Central Asian horseman wearing a conical cap with upturned brim gallops towards the left; his face and torso are, however, facing to the right.

3.2 This block contains a number of scenes. From right to left: three foreigners are engaged in various activities: a turbaned groom leads a horse by the bridle. A horseman brandishes an unsheathed sword in his right. Another groom, probably of Central Asian origin, wearing a pointed cap with a central tassel (?) leads a camel. A tree marks a change of scene: a local man is faced by a tiger emerging from a thicket suggested by two trees. The upraised hands of the figure dramatically convey his helplessness. In the last scene a large monkey, comfortably seated between two trees, eats fruit.

3.3 Faintly etched: A saddled horse, without rider, proceeding at a gallop.

3.4 Two Central Asian horsemen gallop towards the left, while turning their bodies towards the right. Both carry a sword in their raised left hands. Between them is a tree. They wear the usual pointed cap, pigtails, trousers and long jackets.

3.5 Three horses facing to the left. That in the middle bears a Central Asian rider dressed like those in 3.4, wielding a sword. The remaining two horses are riderless.

3.6 Central Asians and horses are the theme of these three scenes. From right to left: a horseman wearing a cap with upturned brim, with a tassel (?) at its centre, flourishes a sword; a riderless horse; a horseman in flowing robes and pointed cap, with a sword in the hand, rides on a horse restrained by a groom.

3.7 Two Central Asian horsemen armed with swords are preceded by a turbaned soldier armed with a round shield and short sword. A shallow scene at the right end of the block shows a tiger elegantly leaping in mid-air.

3.8 A right-facing horse.

3.9 A right-facing horse. The rest of the block is uncarved.

Elephants and Trees

4.1 From right to left: Three elephants facing left: the first wraps his trunk around a tree; the second elephant raises its trunk above a diminutive tree; the third elephant paces majestically.

4.2 Two elephants facing left: the first proceeds towards a tree; the second paces ahead.

4.3 Four elephants facing left. The first elephant moves towards a faintly carved tree; the other three elephants progress to the left.

Chapter Seven

CARVINGS ON THE SOUTH STAIRCASE

As has already been suggested in Chapter 3, the South Staircase affixed to the south face of Phase I should be dated somewhere between Phases I and II. For this reason, the carvings on this part of the monument are described separately.

SOUTH FACE

Narasimha and Chenchu-Lakshmi

Note: All the blocks here are framed by a narrow unsculpted border.

1.1 A beater brandishing a beating-stick in the raised right hand and restraining a huge dog on a leash in his left hand proceeds towards a tree. He is wearing the usual short lower garment, hair tied in a bun, and carefully rendered earrings. To the left of the tree, in the next tableau, is a huntress, probably Chenchu-Lakshmi, armed with a bow and arrow. She is concealed behind an imaginatively rendered tree, shooting arrows at a cluster of animals, mainly gazelles. She is followed by a male figure, probably Narasimha, carrying a dead gazelle over his shoulders. The next scene depicts the cluster of animals at which the huntress aims from her hideout. In the proximity of the animals is a huge monkey, comfortably settled beneath a tree, eating fruit. The next scene illustrates the dramatic encounter between a rearing tiger and a hunter, who thrusts his spear into its chest. A tree separates this scene from the next, which shows two male figures and their dogs. The first figure holds a stick in the right hand; the other figure carries a dead animal over the shoulders. A half-tree concludes this block.

1.2 This block begins with the remaining half of the tree from 1.1, beneath which four gazelles frolic. The feet of one animal rest on a narrow shelf. An elegant rendering of the episode in which Narasimha extracts the thorn from the foot of Chenchu-Lakshmi is prominently placed at the centre of the block. Both the positioning and the quality of the carving indicate that these were especially important images. Chenchu-Lakshmi wears a short-leaf skirt and heavy earrings. She leans gracefully on her bow, which serves as a division between the opening tableau and the rendering of this scene. The sequence of scenes on this block ends with a standing hunter armed with a long stick (or bow?), and the huntress aiming at a boar (in 1.3) from behind a half-tree. It is probable that the couple is Narasimha and Chenchu-Lakshmi. *(Plate 35)*

1.3 The last block of this sequence opens again with a half-tree. Two dogs rush towards a huge boar, rearing on its hind legs, fatally hit by the arrow of the huntress in 1.2. A tree separates this gory scene from an idyllic rendering of forest animals, neatly arranged in two rows, one above the other. Deer, gazelles and does rest their feet on a 'shelf'. A tree concludes this scene. The boar hunt motif is resumed in the next part of the narrative. The animal is attacked by two dogs; one jumps on its back, while the other bites at its throat. Behind a tree, which divides this scene from the next, a huntress aims arrows at a boar. She is accompanied by the usual male figure carrying a dead animal on his shoulders. Three dogs follow the couple. The concluding scene begins with a tree, under which is a dog. The huntress seductively leans, or perhaps stretches her body, on her bow. Her foot rests on the bow, and her tresses have loosened in the heat of the hunt. Opposite her is the hunter with the dead animal on his shoulders. *(Plate 36)*

Decorative Frieze

2.1 to **2.4** Blocks with meandering creeper and hamsa motif. 2.2 introduces hamsas with intertwined necks, and a makara with a creeper sprouting from its mouth. *(Plate 39)*

Music and Dance

3.1 A dancing girl performs with energy, accompanied by two groups of musicians. To her left are two women, one playing a wind instrument, probably a nagasvaram, and the other a vina; to her right, a mridanga-player punctuates the rhythm. The power of the music is such that she gets carried away and dances while beating the drum. The last figure of this group plays the nagasvaram. The second group centres around a dancer who bends backwards so that her head touches her raised right foot. Three musicians, playing nagasvaram, vina and mridanga, stand to the left of this dancer. Two further musicians, with wind and percussion instruments, complete the group to her right. At the end of the block, yet another nagasvaram-player, facing left, introduces the music and dance scenes of 3.2.

3.2 Two mridanga-players accompany a pair of dancing girls. As in 3.1, one of the musicians is carried away by the rhythm and joins in the dance. A second group of four musicians, playing nagasvaram, mridanga and damaru, flank a female dancer shown in the same acrobatic pose as the figure in 3.1; here, however, the dancer touches her head with the left foot. The last scene of the sequence shows a dancer flanked by two mridanga-players and a nagasvaram-player. The dancer and the musicians all wear long flared skirts with elaborate pleated sashes at the front. Their long hair is knotted in heavy buns resting on the napes of their necks. They wear the usual jewellery and conspicuous round earrings.

3.3 Elephant uprooting a shrub and groom (part of the balustrade of the southern staircase, abutting the end of 4.4). The man encourages the animal by gently prodding its hind parts with a pronged staff. This is a superbly crafted block: the head and trunk of the elephant and the shrub are fully carved, while the body of the animal and that of the groom are in low relief, albeit deeply cut.

Stick-Dancers

4.1 The music and dance scenes of this row open with a female musician enthusiastically performing on the nagasvaram. As she stands with feet apart, tense in the exertion of blowing, her body bends diagonally towards a group of stick-dancers on the next block.

4.2 A line of nine stick-dancers gracefully performs to the beat of a mridanga-player. The musician is in a dancing stance, as if carried away by her own music. The dancers are arranged in pairs, so while their bodies confront each other, their heads are turned backwards. This movement is stressed by the positioning of the arms: the stick held in the uplifted right hand of one dancer clashes with that in the raised left hand of the next dancer; at waist level, the stick held in the left hand of the first dancer clashes with that held in the right hand of the second dancer.

4.3 The sequence of dance and music continues. The line of dancers continues uninterrupted from 4.2 to 4.3. Following the arrangement already noted, the first dancer of this block clashes her stick with that held by the last dancer in 4.2, while facing the second dancer in 4.3. Two musicians, one playing the mridanga and the other the trumpet, interrupt the line of dancers, which is then resumed by the last dancer tying in with the first dancer in 4.4.

4.4 This sequence ends with four stick-dancers. This rhythmic arrangement of raised and lowered arms and lightly swinging bodies imparts a meandering movement to this composition. The overall impression is heightened by the costumes of the dancers and musicians, all of whom wear the usual flared skirts with pleated sashes at the front. They also have long pigtails, heavy necklaces and large round earrings.

Vasantotsava Celebrations

5.1 Here begins a sequence of Vasantotsava celebrations. As in 4.1, a group of musicians sets the scene. A trio of ladies playing nagasvaram and mridanga provides the accompaniment. Then come two revellers facing each other across a basin filled with water. With one hand they scoop water from the basin; in the other hand they possibly carry a small cup, which their raise in a mockingly defiant gesture. The next two figures are shown singing and dancing; the figure to the right clearly carries a small cup in the raised hand. In the next scene a woman and man, both with plaits, energetically scoop water from a basin placed between them. The man is interrupted by the sudden intervention of a woman embracing him from behind. While she is thus occupied, her companion, the last figure in this scene, pulls her plaited hair. *(Plate 41)*

5.2 Two women with uplifted arms, possibly singing, look at two other women busily filling their small containers from a basin placed between them. They are shown exactly in the same stance as the figures in 5.1. Two mridanga-players in dancing pose and a nagasvaram-player lifting her head and her instrument conclude this sequence of Vasantotsava celebrations.

5.3 This may not form an original part of the balustrade. Early photographs of the monument show this block missing; it was found fallen nearby. A composite figure consists of a man with three heads, four arms and four legs. Adjacent to this figure is a partly three-dimensional sculpture of a fierce, open-mouthed yali, its right forepaw menacingly raised. At its feet crouches a makara, with its head bent backwards. The trunks of the two animals are interlocked. From the open mouth of the makara issues an elegant cascade of foliage. On the rear face of the balustrade, behind the relief of the composite male figure, is an imposing Central Asian chowkidar leaning pensively on his long staff with both hands. This bearded figure is clad in a long flowing robe and wears a small cap with upturned brim.

Decorative Frieze

6.1 and **6.2** Frieze of meandering creeper with hamsas. At either end of the frieze is a decorative shape reminiscent of a seed or a pot, from which originates a creeper. The two creepers merge in an ornate foliage knot at the centre of the frieze.

Elephants, Trees and Horsemen

7.1 Elephants and mahouts. The first elephant is ridden by a diminutive mahout, who covers his head with a blanket. The animal wraps his trunk around a tall palm tree, on which perches a monkey. A second elephant is shown in a similar manner; however, instead of a monkey, a squirrel scurries up the trunk of the palm-tree. A third elephant is preceded by a mahout with a forked staff resting on his shoulder, with which he rips the foliage off a crown of a tree inhabited by several birds. The fourth elephant happily eats the leaves of a palm tree. Yet another tree divides this animal from a fifth elephant, also shown eating the leaves of a palm-tree. A tree inhabited by two parrots, shown back to back, preening their feathers (see Phase I, west part, south face 3.1), introduces the final scene. Here an elephant with a tiny mahout precariously seated on its back is watered by a groom, pouring water from a crescent-shaped basin placed before it. A pacing elephant concludes the block. *(Plates 43 to 45)*

7.2 Two horsemen, probably Central Asian, ride at full speed on rearing horses. The panel, possibly misplaced, is damaged and weathered; the details are no longer discernible. *(Plate 45)*

EAST FACE

Forest Scenes and the Story of Narasimha Wooing Chenchu-Lakshmi

All the blocks are framed on four sides.

1.1 A huntress concealed behind a tree aims at two antelopes. The two animals fight, interlocking their horns, on the backdrop of a tree with a sumptuous crown. The next scene, separated from the previous one by a tree, shows animals roaming in the forest. They include three gazelles, one of which flees from the huntress's dogs, which attack a boar, rearing on his hind legs. A tree partly conceals the huntress, the two dogs and her male companion carrying a dead animal on his shoulders. The huntress aims an arrow at the boar. At this point, the forest sequence is interrupted by Chenchu-Lakshmi leaning gracefully on her bow, with the left leg elegantly poised on it. The following tableau depicts Narasimha kneeling, while extracting a thorn from Chenchu-Lakshmi's foot. A tree marks the end of this scene. The forest sequence is resumed with the depiction of a hunter carrying a dead animal on his shoulder, preceded by the huntress behind a tree aiming arrows at a bear rearing on its hind legs facing towards her. *(Plate 37)*

1.2 A bear, facing to the left, rearing on its hind legs. *(Plate 38)*

Decorative Frieze

2.1 and **2.2** As on the south face the second row is occupied by a frieze of meandering creepers and hamsas. The creepers issue from the mouth of a makara concealed among the foliage in 2.2. *(Plate 38)*

Dance and Music

3.1 A continuation of the dance and music scenes in the third row of south face. A female orchestra consisting of three nagasvaram-players, two vina-players and four mridanga-players provides the accompaniment for a performance by four dancers. The second dancer from the right exhibits her acrobatic skills by bending backwards so as to touch her head with her raised foot. (See also 3.1 and 3.2 on the south face.)

3.2 Two dancers, a vina-player and a young acrobat walking on her hands with her feet resting on her head perform before a courtly figure. He is seated in a relaxed attitude on a throne, with his right elbow leaning on a bolster, holding a flower (?) in the left hand. His left leg is crossed over his right leg and rests on the seat; his right leg hangs down. His hair is tied in a bun on the nape of the neck. The details of the costume are not very clear: probably he wears a knee-length, lower garment and is bare-chested. The musicians and dancers wear long flared skirts with elaborate pleated sashes at the front. Their long hair is tied in heavy buns resting on the napes of the necks. They wear the usual jewellery and conspicuous round earrings. *(Plate 42)*

3.3 Two female attendants, a chauri-bearer and a sword-bearer stand behind the seated courtly figure. The chauri held by the attendant, spills over into 3.2.

Stick-Dancers

4.1 Continuation of the dance sequence on the south face. This composition opens with the spirited rendering of a nagasvaram-player. She is followed by five graceful stick-dancers, similar to those on the south face (4.1 to 4.4). The last dancer on this block forms a pair with the first dancer of 4.2.

4.2 The first dancer completes the group shown in 4.2. A mridanga-player ushers in a group of nine stick-dancers, the last forming a pair with the mridanga-player, the last but one figure in the block. A nagasvaram-player concludes the group. *(Plate 42)*

Vasantotsava Celebrations

5.1 This forms part of the Vasantotsava celebrations sequence on the fifth row on the south face. This small block depicts a wind-instrument player facing left.

5.2 The celebrations open with a mridanga-player accompanying the water play and dances. At the centre of the composition are Kama, armed with bow and arrow, and Rati, hanging onto his arm. To the left of Kama is a woman with raised arms. The trio is flanked by two groups of women armed with squirts, four to the right, and five to the left. Basins filled with water are placed between them at regular intervals.

5.3 The row ends with this small block with a figure of a woman carrying a squirt.

Decorative Frieze

6.1 Continuation of the frieze on the sixth row of the south face. This single, large block has a frieze of meandering creepers, each enclosing a hamsa issuing from the mouth of a makara, in the middle.

Elephant, Trees and Formal Reception

7.1 Several of these scenes are similar to that on the seventh row of south face. An elephant uproots a shrub at the foot of a tree, followed by another elephant in the same attitude. In the foliage of the second tree are two parrots depicted back to back (see south face 7.1). A third elephant carrying two diminutive riders plunges its trunk in the crown of a tree. A fourth elephant wraps its trunk around a tree; a fifth elephant picks the foliage from yet another tree while a squirrel scuttles up its stem. At this point the scenes change abruptly from a rural to a courtly setting. Two Central Asian visitors, clad in typical flowing robes, one wearing a cap with upturned brim, and the other a tight-fitting cap, are granted audience by three noblemen seated together on a seat. The first nobleman, with his left leg crossed over the right leg, which hangs loosely from the seat, rests his elbow on a bolster. The remaining two noblemen sit cross-legged on the seat. (This composition may be compared with that on Phase I, south face, west part, 2.5.) All the noblemen have their long hair tied in buns. They wear knee-length, lower garments, and are probably bare-chested.

7.2 A chowkidar, dressed in a knee-length, lower garment, leans on a staff propped under his right arm. He sports a conspicuous moustache, a triangular beard and a small cap. Possibly he wears a neck ornament and a sword may hang from his waist. His legs are shown frontally, while his torso and head are rendered in profile. The most striking feature of this figure is the face, with large, pensive eyes gazing towards a distant point to the left.

Balustrade

Outer (south) Face From right to left: Composite three-headed, four-legged and four-armed figure; and a large elephant-headed yali, whose trunk is joined with that of a makara, squatting in front of it. A shrub issues from the makara's mouth. *(Plates 46 and 47)*

Inner (north) Face From right to left: A yali; and a central Asian chowkidar leaning on staff. *(Plates 48 and 49)*

Steps

Middle Series Third step (from the top). A monkey standing on the back of a bird. The scene is defined by a tree on each side. This may be an illustration of a folk tale. *(Plate 50)*

Top Series The first step (from the top) shows a meandering creeper. The second step (from the top) has two blocks: one displays a meandering creeper; the other a fragment of a meandering creeper and hamsa/mayura motifs. The third step (from the top) has two blocks depicting a scene of music and dance, probably a fragment of a Vasantotsava celebrations sequence. On the carvings are three female musicians playing the mridanga, tambourine and nagasvaram. They shown with a fourth woman with a long pigtail holding a cup in her raised hand.

Chapter Eight

CARVINGS OF PHASE II

SOUTH FACE

Second Row

2A and **2B** Reliefs on a boulder (damaged). A right-facing horseman is welcomed by two figures; two men ride on an elephant towards the left. *(Plate 51)*

2.1 to **2.5** Blank.

2.6 Foliage motif, or possibly branches of a tree, enlivened by a monkey and a bird. This block constitutes the lower part of 4.19.

2.7 A hunter wearing the usual knee-length, lower garment, with the hair tied at the nape of his neck, aims an arrow at two jumping gazelles. In the foreground is a third animal, perhaps a boar.

2.8 Animals copulating in a forest. A dog (?) performs oral sex on a gazelle, which, in turn, is having anal intercourse with another animal. A tree to the left completes the scene.

2.9 Blank.

2.10 A hamsa/mayura carrying a twig in its beak is inscribed in a medallion.

2.11 Blank.

2.12 A left-facing elephant uproots a tree.

2.13 A warrior, armed with sword and shield. The man wears an elaborate headgear, resembling to a turban.

2.14 Unfinished carving, possibly a mridanga-player.

2.15 and **2.16** Blank.

2.17 A visual pun: four monkeys with two heads and four bodies.

2.18 to **2.20** Blank.

2.21 Unfinished: a huntress clad in the typical foliage skirt, wearing a crown of leaves stretches her elegant body, holding on to a bow.

2.22 Unfinished: two female dancers.

2.23 to 2.30 Blank.

2.31 A seated animal, perhaps a monkey.

2.32 and **2.33** Blank.

Third Row

Narrow frames run along one or more edges of many of the blocks.

3.1 A local horseman on a horse facing left. This and the following scene can be seen as a narrative sequence. The lower parts of this block as well as 3.2 and 3.3 are concealed by modern paving slabs.

3.2 A royal figure seated in the typical pose, a chauri-bearer standing in attendance behind the throne, and a 'master of ceremonies' carrying a staff, all facing to the right, welcome the horseman in 3.1.

3.3 A Central Asian groom, badly damaged, leads a horse.

3.4 An elephant wraps its trunk around a tree (defaced).

3.5 Two running men are armed with sticks or spears; they carry unidentified objects in their left hands.

3.6 A horseman on a left-facing, galloping horse, brandishes an unsheathed sword in the left hand and looks back towards 3.5. Possibly 3.5 and 3.6 form a narrative sequence.

3.7 and **3.8** A complex forest scene, forming part of 4.15. In 3.7, a gazelle, tiger and boar roam in a forest. Part of the boar's body extends into 3.8. Here a dog barks at a tiger climbing the trunk of a tree, while yet another tiger, hangs horizontally from its branches. *(Plate 56)*

3.9 Two hunters, each armed with a bow, look in opposite directions. The arm of the left-facing man into 3.10, may suggest a connection between the two scenes.

3.10 A seated royal figure, with a chauri-bearer standing behind, receives a man carrying an unidentified object in his hands.

3.11 A horse shaded by a parasol. It is probable that the depicted animal is the 'state horse' that played a major role in courtly functions. The figure of the groom that leads it has almost disappeared.

3.12 Unfinished (?): a bird.

3.13 Two scenes: On the right, a deeply cut standing woman carries a string instrument, possibly a vina. On the left is a crudely carved hunter aiming arrows at the animals in 3.14. The two carvings are separated by a plain, pilaster-like element.

3.14 Three gazelles, two of which are jumping, one grazing, and three (?) additional animals. The shallow relief in which the carvings are executed makes the identification of the animals difficult.

3.15 A superbly carved tree full of fruit, with monkeys inhabiting its densely foliated crown. One animal sits, fruit in hand, sits at the base of the tree. The remainder of the scene has diverse animals; in the foreground are a tiger and a boar; in the background are copulating boars with their feet resting on a 'ledge'.

3.16 Two hunters facing right: One hunter, armed with a bow and two arrows, is followed by a dog; the other hunter has just shot an arrow towards the animals in the forest carved on 3.15, which forms part of the same narrative sequence.

3.17 Partly defaced. A cluster of animals: a tiger, two leaping gazelles, and a waterbird (?).

3.18 A tiger attacks a gazelle (?), a dog pounces on the wounded animal, and another gazelle jumps away.

3.19 Two leaping gazelles facing opposite directions.

3.20 A beater and a hunter aim arrows at the gazelles depicted in 3.19. Possibly 3.17 to 3.20 form part of the same sequence.

3.21 An elephant pacing towards the left.

3.22 A wrestling match. One of the figures has knotted himself around the adversary. A third man is warming up at the side. The wrestlers wear knee-length, lower garments and their long hair is tied in buns at the backs of their head. *(Plate 54)*

3.23 A group of four wrestlers. Three wrestlers are shown on a platform in various attitudes: one sits on the floor in a pensive mood; the two next to him are involved in a match, and the one to the extreme left, off stage, warms up. All the men wear tight-fitting caps (?).

3.24 A tiger (?) jumps on the rump of a pacing elephant.

3.25 Two Central Asian figures, dressed in typical long cloaks and tiered pointed caps and long pigtails, stand holding hands. *(Plate 53)*

3.26 A seated personage, possibly a Central Asian ruler or dignitary, dressed in the same attire as in 3.25, hands a necklace (?) to a Central Asian trader. Interestingly, the depiction of the foreign ruler or dignitary is inspired by that of the royal figure. Probably 3.25 and 3.26 form a narrative sequence. *(Plate 53)*

3.27 A man sits beneath a tree, his right leg crossed over the left. In his hand he carries an unidentified object, possibly a rosary. *(Plate 53)*

3.28 A man runs carrying an unidentified object in his raised right hand.

3.29 A natha (?), his right leg firmly held by a yogapatta while his left leg dangles down, rides on a fabulous animal with a lion's head. *(Plate 60)*

3.30 This rather weathered block shows two men engaged in an animated conversation. One, obviously a courtly figure sits on a low seat, his right leg resting on it, his left leg hanging down. The other man stands opposite him.

3.31 A royal figure sits on a stepped throne, his left leg crossed over the right leg. His left elbow rests on a round bolster, while his right arm lies on the right knee. His carefully rendered hair bun, resting at the nape of the neck, is now almost completely obliterated. An attendant, with raised right hand that probably once bore a chauri, stands behind him. Both figures face to the left.

3.32 A horseman, brandishing a sword in his left hand, rides at full gallop towards the left. His head, however, is turned towards the right.

3.33 A richly caparisoned elephant, majestically moving towards the left, uproots a shrub.

3.34 An elephant, on whose side is carved a peacock grooming its tail, walks unperturbed carrying a tiger on its back. The elephant faces to the right, and the tiger to the left. *(Plate 59)*

3.35 A spirited gazelle leaps through the forest, suggested by a single tree. Since the block is very narrow the artists inventively carved the animal along the diagonal of the block. *(Plates 58 and 59)*

3.36 A deeply cut female figure with a parrot perched on her left hand is set in a niche, perhaps suggesting a door. She is flanked by imposing male figures, probably chowkidars, carved in shallow relief. The one to the left, a Central Asian, judging from his cap and pigtail, leans on a staff; the one to the right rests his staff on the left shoulder. The impressive size of the men contrasts with the slight figure of the woman. *(Plate 58)*

Fourth Row

Narrow frames run along one or more edges of many of the blocks.

4.1 Two men conversing, with a diminutive tree in between. The figure on the right hands something to the man opposite. The next scene represents a horse being paraded by a Central Asian groom clad like those in 3.25 and 3.26. The last scene shows a gatekeeper in flowing robes, probably also a Central Asian, leaning on his staff, ushering a visitor into the presence of a seated royal figure. Both the gatekeeper and visitor wear coats with long sleeves covering the hands. The lower portions of this block as well as those of 4.2, 4.3 and 4.4 have been partly obscured by modern paving slabs. *(Plate 52)*

4.2 This block, part of the series of scenes in 4.1, shows a chauri-bearer standing behind a seated royal figure.

4.3 A Central Asian horseman, brandishing a sword, proceeds at a gallop. He is preceded by a turbaned soldier, as noted in 2.13, armed with sword and shield.

4.4 A local horseman on a galloping horse. The rider turns his head towards the right. Possibly 4.3 and 4.4 form a sequence.

4.5 A tree and a camel pacing towards the left.

4.6 A camel proceeding towards the left.

4.7 An elephant progressing towards the left.

4.8 A tree with a lush crown fills the whole block.

4.9 A left-facing elephant.

4.10 A forest scene, partly damaged. Enclosed between two trees at the ends of the block is a pacing elephant. A monkey sits in the crown of the tree to the left, while another monkey climbs on its trunk.

4.11 Inserted block: a tree.

4.12 An elephant and a half-elephant proceed towards to the left.

4.13 The remaining half of the elephant of 4.12, and another full animal proceeds towards the left. This block and the previous blocks constitute a narrative unit.

4.14 Visual pun: gajavrishabha. A composite elephant and bull (compare with Phase I, south face, west part, 6.9).

4.15 A hunter stands in the crown of a tree, bow in one hand and sword in the other. From here he kills a tiger by thrusting his sword in its mouth. Parts of this same scene are also found on 3.7 and 3.8. *(Plate 56)*

4.16 Part of the foliage of the tree shown in 4.15 extends into this block. An elephant wraps its trunk around a tree carved onto the left-hand portion of the block.

4.17 The theme of the elephant wrapping its trunk around a tree is repeated here.

4.18 The same motif as in 4.16 and 4.17. In all the three blocks elephants are shown with upraised tails.

4.19 A scene divided into two registers: in the upper register an elephant wraps its trunk around a tree; in the lower register a bird and monkey are set among foliage. See also 2.6.

4.20 A scene divided into two registers: in the upper register is a left-facing peacock; in the lower register there are two dogs (?)

4.21 Two scenes: to the right a hamsa/mayura holding a twig in its beak; to the left an unfinished figure seated in what could possibly be a cave. A tree and duck (?), both carved in shallow relief, constitute the foreground of this unusual scene.

4.22 This weathered scene depicts three left-facing soldiers armed with swords and shields.

4.23 This weathered scene depicts a groom leading a saddled horse towards the left.

4.24 Five men wielding long spears march towards the left.

4.25 Two wrestlers engaged in a match. To the right, a third wrestler is shown warming up. The men wear the usual short lower garments; their hair is covered with tight fitting caps (?).

4.26 A royal figure sits on the throne, his left leg crossed over his right leg; his left hand raised. Behind him stands a chauri-bearer, with a sword-bearer stands in front. It is probable that this scene forms a single unit with 4.25.

4.27 Two men seated, their left legs resting on a platform and their right legs hanging down, look towards the royal figure in 4.28.

4.28 A seated, bearded royal figure a chauri-bearer in attendance. A 'master of ceremonies' standing before him points with his staff to the wrestlers in 4.29.

4.29 Two wrestlers (?). One pays obeisance with folded hands to the seated royal figure to the right noted in 4.28; the other, covering his face with his hands, faces left. Both wrestlers carry clubs (?) under their arms.

4.30 Two wrestlers engaged in a match; a third performing gymnastic exercises. 4.27 to 4.30 form a continuous narrative sequence.

4.31 Weathered panel: tree with birds.

4.32 A seated monkey holds a snake in its hand. A tree concludes the blocks on the right.

4.33 A local groom leads a horse.

4.34 Composite figure: a man with three heads, four arms and four legs. The same motif, only on a larger scale is carved on the South Staircase (south face 5.3).

4.35 A left-facing horse, proceeding at a pace.

4.36 A left-facing elephant.

4.37 A left-facing elephant, sumptuously caparisoned.

4.38 A left-facing 'state horse' in full trappings, profusely decorated, shaded by a parasol (compared 3.11 and 4.40). *(Plate 55)*

4.39 Two seated monkeys eating fruit of the tree standing between them. *(Plate 60)*

4.40 A left-facing 'state horse' in full trappings, profusely decorated, and shaded by a parasol. See also 3.11 and 4.38.

4.41 A richly caparisoned elephant carries a shrub (?) in its trunk.

4.42 A man carrying a pole from which hangs a yak-tail (?), possibly a royal insignia.

4.43 A standing warrior, facing to the right, armed with sword and shield.

4.44 An elephant carries shrubs or foliage in its trunk.

4.45 A standing warrior facing to the left, armed with sword and shield.

4.46 A rider on a left-facing galloping horse turns back to look above his shoulder.

4.47 A rider, brandishing an unsheathed sword, proceeds to the left at a gallop.

Fifth Row

Narrow frames run along one or more edges of many of the blocks.

5.1 An elephant progresses towards the left.

5.2 A left-facing elephant walks towards the tree carved onto 5.3, the crown of which extends into 5.3.

5.3 A tree, a left-facing elephant, and a half-tree.

5.4 The second half of the tree noted in 5.3 and a left-facing elephant. It is probable that 5.1 to 5.4 form a single unit.

5.5 A left-facing camel.

5.6 A left-facing elephant.

5.7 A left-facing elephant.

5.8 A Central Asian groom leads a horse. An elephant concludes the scene to the left. The carving is executed in shallow relief.

5.9 A Central Asian guest, dressed as the figures in 3.25 and 3.26, is granted audience with a seated courtly figure. The latter carries a sword in his right and rests it on his shoulder. A local door-keeper leaning on his staff stands between the seated figure and the foreign visitor.

5.10 A left-facing, tethered (?) horse.

5.11 A horseman riding a galloping horse proceeds towards the left.

5.12 A tree and a left-facing elephant.

5.13 A right-facing horse.

5.14 Damaged block. A left-facing elephant.

5.15 Damaged block. A right-facing horse.

5.16 A Central Asian horseman with raised right arm rides towards the left. A tree defines the block to the right.

5.17 A horseman, brandishing a weapon (?) in his raised right hand, rides towards the right.

5.18 A Central Asian trader (?), clad in a long cloak, parades a horse leading it by the bridle.

5.19 A Central Asian horseman, carrying a long spear rides in a forested landscape suggested by two trees carved at both ends of the block. The tree to the left extends onto 5.20.

5.20 A local groom leads a horse by the bridle beneath a tree.

5.21 An archer rides at full speed towards the left, while at the same moment aiming his arrows towards the right.

5.22 Three elephants: The first two animals wrap their trunks around a tree; a third elephant proceeds towards the left.

5.23 A caparisoned elephant proceeds towards the left.

5.24 A right-facing elephant.

5.25 A left-facing caparisoned elephant.

5.26 A man thrusts his dagger into the neck of a tiger. In this rather crude carving the man seems to place his knee on the spine of the animal to break it by violently tugging its tail.

5.27 A left-facing elephant.

5.28 A left-facing elephant.

5.29 A left-facing elephant wraps his trunk around a tree.

5.30 A horseman riding towards the left.

5.31 A long-cloaked, Central Asian groom leads a horse.

5. 32 A Central Asian groom dressed as noted in 5.31 leads two horses. The group is preceded by an elephant with local groom carrying a staff on his shoulder.

Sixth Row

Here, too, narrow frames run along one or more edges of many of the blocks.

6.1 Hamsa in meandering creeper motif. A frame runs along the upper and lower edges of the block. This motif is similar to that noted on the South Staircase (south and east faces, rows 2 and 6).

6.2 to 6.5 Hamsas in meandering creeper motifs.

6.6 Hamsa in meandering creeper motif. The motif ends roughly in the middle of the block. Along with it ceases the frames along the top and bottom edges of the block. The left-hand portion accommodates two birds with two heads each and a peacock (?).

6.7 Four left-facing, strutting peacocks.

6.8 Three Central Asian horsemen, brandishing swords, proceed at a gallop to the left.

6.9 A heron (?) and three peacocks proceed towards the left. The second peacock is endowed with two heads.

6.10 Damaged block. Of the original six peacocks only four can be made, two at either end of the block, all facing to the left.

6.11 Five left-facing peacocks.

WEST FACE, SOUTH PART

Narrow frames run along one or more edges of many of the blocks.

Second Row

2.1 Hamsas with intertwined necks.

2.2 Concealed by the plastered concrete floor.

2.3 Partly concealed: two left-facing birds and a flower (or a branch).

2.4 Partly concealed: a left-facing bird.

2.5 Partly concealed: a left-facing peacock.

2.6 A left-facing two-headed duck (?).

2.7 Two left-facing, water-birds among foliage (?) or flowers (?).

2.8 A left-facing bird pecks its foot.

2.9 A peacock (?) preens its plumage. The body of the bird is oriented towards the left, but the head faces right.

2.10 A right-facing duck, partly obscured.

Third Row

3.1 A man talks to a door-keeper leaning on his long staff.

3.2 An elephant proceeds towards the left.

3.3 A large tree, the crown filling practically the whole block, is inhabited by monkeys and birds.

3.4 A seated, large monkey holds a fruit (?) in its hands. It is surrounded by four smaller monkeys: two climb onto the tail and rump of the large monkey; another perches on a nearby tree; the last stands near the tree trunk.

3.5 A large tree with two monkey perched in a branch. Another monkey one sits at its base.

3.6 A hunter, concealed behind a tree, aims arrows at a group of wild animals, including a gazelle and boar. The animals are rendered as if standing one above the other; however, a small 'ledge' beneath their feet suggests that each stands on the ground. The size of the hunter dwarfs the animals.

3.7 A left-facing elephant wraps its trunk a tree.

3.8 Three two-headed, water-birds in a forested landscape.

3.9 In the right-hand portion of the block a beater with the usual stick, accompanied by a dog on the leash, heads towards a clearing in the forest. A tree, a lively rendering of a boar grazing, and various gazelles fleeing the approaching man occupy the remainder of the scene.

3.10 Partly concealed: a groom brushes the head of a horse.

Fourth Row

4.1 In the right-hand portion two buffaloes facing left are confronted by a tiger. The buffalo in the foreground has lowered its head, as if preparing to charge the tiger; the second buffalo, almost totally concealed behind it, raises its head looking towards the right. The forested landscape is suggested by a diminutive tree placed between the tiger and buffaloes. A second tree divides this scene from that in the left-hand portion. Here a Central Asian groom leads a horse by the bridle.

4.2 A horseman, with his left hand raised, rides a left-facing prancing horse.

4.3 An elephant paces towards the left.

4.4 An elephant paces towards the left.

4.5 A monkey pulls at the end of the sari of a woman paying homage to an ascetic. The ascetic, depicted frontally, wears a conical cap; his hands rest on a staff; a conspicuous yoga-patta keeps his knees firmly in position.

4.6 A man, armed with a spear, transfixes a rearing tiger. A gazelle leaps in between the man and tiger.

4.7 A man thrusts a dagger into the neck of a lion. The face of the animal is strongly reminiscent of that of the 'squatting lion' commonly seen at the base of temple pillars.

4.8 A left-facing elephant wraps its trunk around a tree.

4.9 Inserted block. Blank.

4.10 A hunter standing at the foot of a tree aims an arrow at a tiger perched on its branches, piercing its mouth. From a safe distance the hunter's dog barks frantically at the scene.

4.11 A tiger (?) paces beneath a tree.

4.12 An elephant carrying foliage in its trunk walks to the left.

4.13 A forest suggested by two trees, between which a tiger sits.

4.14 Concealed.

Top Row

6.1 to **6.3** Blank.

WEST FACE, NORTH PART

Narrow frames run along the edges of all the blocks.

Fifth Row

5.83 Partly obscured: left-facing peacock (?).

5.84 Two horses facing each other: one canters; the other rubs its nose against its foreleg.

5.85 A left-facing prancing horse. Behind it is a tree.

5.86 Two peacocks facing each other groom the feathers on their back. Their heads are turned towards the left and towards the right, respectively.

5.87 A tree is carved at either end of the block. Beneath each tree is a bird pecking something from its branches. The birds' bodies face each other, but their heads are depicted in opposite directions.

5.88 A peacock (?) grooms the plumage on its back. Its body is oriented towards the left, the head, however, faces to the right. A tree concludes the block to the north.

5.89 Two ducks, arranged back to back, twist their heads so as to stare at each other.

5.90 A left-facing peacock pecks its foot.

5.91 A long-beaked, water bird picks something from a plant.

5.92 Two peacocks with intertwined necks. A tree is carved at either end of the block.

5.93 A two-headed bird: one head bends forward pecking at its foot; the other head faces to the right. A tree delimits the left-hand end of the scene.

5.94 A peacock (?) grooms the feathers on its back: the body is oriented towards the left, and the head towards the right. A tree or a shrub concludes the scene to the left.

5.95 A bird picks something from the branch of a tree.

5.96 Blank.

5.97 A bird between two trees.

5.98 A woman carries a tray with arati lamps and a bell. She looks towards the ascetic in 5.99.

5.99 An ascetic (?) with a staff resting on the right shoulder and a kapala (?) in the left hand. He looks towards the woman in 5.98.

5.100 Matsyendranath seated on a fish. His arm rests on a staff and his legs are tied with a yogapatta. While the fish faces towards the left, the ascetic faces in the opposite direction. Probably 5.98 to 5.100 form a narrative sequence.

Top Row

6.95 A right-facing groom, leading a horse by the bridle. The scene is partly obscured by Phase IV.

6.96 The left-hand portion of the scene shows an imposing hunter concealed behind a tree, aiming an arrow at the gaping mouth of a tiger. The animal, hit in the mouth, rears on its hind legs. Gazelles, docs, boars and other animals flee helter-skelter. A two-headed buffalo occupies the right-hand portion of the scene; one head of the animal faces to the right; with the other head it licks its hind leg. A tree and a right-facing horse complete the scene.

6.97 An enraged elephant has caught hold of a groom. The left leg of the man is caught in the trunk of the animal, which tramples upon his right leg. With its hind legs it crushes another groom, who tries desperately to escape. Three men armed with forked staffs attempt to restrain the beast. *(Plate 62)*

6.98 Two scenes are separated by a narrow, plain vertical band. The right-hand scene completes the composition in 6.97. Here, two men brandishing forked staffs rush towards an enraged elephant. The left-hand scene shows a royal figure seated on a low throne, flanked by a chauri-bearer and conversing with a door-keeper leaning on his staff. A boxer, dressed in a short lower garment and with the hair protected by a tight fitting cap, pays homage to him. The last part of this scene shows a boxing match in progress.

6.99 A buffalo charges a growling tiger, which emerges from behind a tree. In the background, unmindful of the tiger, an elephant plunges its trunk into the crown of a tree.

6.100 Two monkeys pick the fruit of a tree, the crown and branches of which fill the whole composition.

NORTH FACE

Elephants

6.1 Damaged block. An elephant proceeds towards the left.

6.2 Damaged block. An enraged elephant (see also west face, north part, 6.97) is pursued by two (?) grooms armed with long staffs. A third man is trampled upon by the mad animal.

6.3 to **6.14** Blank.

EAST FACE

4.88 and **4.89** Blank.

Forest and Hunting Scenes

4.90 A hunter aims an arrow at a cluster of gazelles. Several unleashed dogs chase the animals, two of which lie dead on the ground. In the background, a third gazelle jumps away.

4.91 A hunter is confronted by a rearing tiger, suddenly appearing from behind a palm (?) tree. The man kills the leaping animal by thrusting a sword deep into its throat. A decoratively rendered tree concludes the panel to the right. To the left, immediately behind the hunter, branches of a tree extend onto 4.92.

4.92 Three trees define various scenes. The right-hand scene, as already noted, is linked with that in 4.91. Beneath its branches are a hunter and his dog proceeding towards the middle of the composition, where a group of wild animals occupies a space defined by two trees. The animals are unaware of the hunter and dog, and graze peacefully. However, one animal with two heads, one bent downwards to the grass, has the other head raised in alert, gazing in the direction of the hunter. An unidentified animal, possibly a bear, is prominently shown in the foreground; a gazelle jumps in the background. A third tree concludes this scene. The next phase of action introduces a hunter, who purposefully strides towards the left. *(Plate 57)*

4.93 Five animals graze in a forest clearing. As in 4.92, none of the animals, except the two-headed gazelle, carved at the left-hand end of the scene, are aware of the impending peril. Three animals in the foreground eat contentedly; a fourth leaps in the background.

4.94 A tree serves as a backdrop to a dramatic scene in which a man kills a leaping tiger by plunging a dagger into its chest. This concludes the sequence of hunting scenes that commenced 4.90.

4.95 Two monkeys sit facing each other, gesticulating animatedly.

4.96 An unidentified grazing animal (a bear?) faces right.

4.97 A herd of gazelles and a boar move towards the right. Two of the gazelles turn their heads towards the left, the direction from which a hunter approaches. Only his bow is shown in this scene.

4.98 The right-hand portion of this scene is occupied by a hunter shooting at the animals in 4.97. The left-hand portion shows a man armed with a huge spear transfixing a tiger in 4.99. A tree extends across into 4.99.

4.99 A huge growling tiger, with teeth bared, approaches a tree behind which the man with the long spear is concealed. A tree on the left concluding the scene extends into 4.100.

4.100 A contemplative man sits at the foot of a tree, gazing to the right towards the tree sculpted across 4.99 and 4.100. A monkey frolics among its branches; another monkey sits beneath the tree eating a fruit.

Horses and Elephants

5.91 The right-hand portion of this scene is unsculpted. In the left-hand portion a turbaned soldier armed with a curved sword and round shield (see south face, 2.13). The soldier proceeds towards the left, though he faces towards the right. Due to the poor condition of the block, the details of the costume are no longer visible.

5.92 A soldier, similar in attire and stance to the one noted in 5.91, progresses towards the left, but looks to the right. A narrow plain vertical band to the left of the figure shows the rump of a horse. The scene continues into 5.93. Due to the poor state of the block, the details are no longer visible.

5.93 Remainder of the horse noted in 5.92. The animal is paraded by a local groom. A second groom, now defaced, leads another horse by the bridle.

5.94 Two horses one without a rider, the other with a rider with raised right arm. Probably 5.91 to 5.94 form a sequence.

5.95 Matsyendranatha seated on a huge fish. The fish faces to the left, while the saint faces to the right. The figure at the right-hand end of the scene here disappeared.

5.96 A left-facing horse.

5.97 A left-facing elephant wraps its trunk around a tree. Another tree to the right delimits the scene.

5.98 A left-facing elephant uproots shrubs.

5.99 A tree inhabited by monkeys. Damaged block.

5.100 A series of figures and animals: a groom curbs a rearing horse; an elephant wraps its trunk around a tree; a left-facing horse and a tree; a left-facing elephant uproots shrubs.

6.9 to **6.12** Hamsas in meandering creeper motifs.

Chapter Nine

CARVINGS OF PHASE III

SOUTH FACE

Lower Upana (Course 2)

2.1 Eight panels defined by pilaster motifs. The first four panels each show an elephant uprooting shrubs. The fifth panel depicts a rider on a horse. The theme of the elephant at work, uprooting shrubs, is resumed in the last three panels. All the figures move towards the left. *(Plate 63)*

2.2 Three panels are defined by a plain unsculpted band, or occasionally by a crudely carved pilaster motif. In the first panel a horseman riding a prancing horse brandishes a spear in his raised right hand. The man moves towards the right, where three vertical lines issuing from a basement may suggest a building or a wall. Two further horsemen are carved onto this block. Both are riding towards the left. The second from the right, an archer, with a dramatic twist of the body aims an arrow towards the right. The second flourishes a sword in the raised right hand.

2.3 Ten panels with the usual pilaster motifs. Varied themes are illustrated here. The first three panels depict elephants. All the animals are facing to the left. The first elephant paces majestically and its trunk spills onto the divisional pilaster; two figures ride on the back of the second elephant, and a third figure is caught in its trunk. The third elephant is depicted walking. The fourth panel shows a huntress carrying in her right hand a tall bow, an arrow in her left hand. She stands elegantly with one foot in front of the other and gazes towards the right. The next four panels depict walking elephants. The last but one panel shows a horseman proceeding at a gallop, holding an unsheathed sword in his raised right hand. The series of panels is concluded by an unfinished female figure with a raised arm, perhaps dancing.

2.4 Eight panels separated by the usual pilaster motifs, showing eight elephants proceeding towards the left.

2.5 Nine panels separated by the usual pilaster motifs. With the exception of the sixth panel, all the animals face to the left. The first panel depicts an elephant with the raised trunk, spilling onto the partition pilaster; the second panel has a horse led by a diminutive groom; in the third and fourth panels the theme of the elephant with the trunk encroaching on the division pillar is repeated. The central, fifth panel accommodates a dancing girl and female mridanga-player performing animatedly. The sixth panel resumes the theme of the elephant with its raised trunk encroaching on the division pillar. In this case, however, the elephant faces to the right. The seventh panel shows a horseman on a richly caparisoned horse, galloping with upraised right hand. The last two panels, both showing elephants, are damaged. The eighth panel depicts an elephant struggling to loose its chain; the ninth panel is destroyed.

2.6 This block is exceptional, since it has no divisions between the scenes and the carvings are not as carefully laid out. There are five elephants, the last partly obscured by the extension on the western face. All the animals face to the left. The first scene depicts an elephant with its trunk wrapped around a tree. The carving is partly damaged. The second elephant is tied to a pole by its hind leg, trying to free itself. This scene is delimited by a rough plain band on the top and on the left side. The remaining two scenes and a fragment of the third scene show progressing elephants.

Gala (Course 6)

(Plates 63 and 74 to 79)

The panels in this course are separated from one another by shallow pilasters.

1 Architectural facade consisting of a pair of split-pilasters with double capitals and a pyramidal roof flanked by upturned petals/nagas (?), with a decorative band on the architrave. Lotus flower motif constituted by a central bud surrounded by two concentric circles of 16 internal and eight external petals. A 16-petalled lotus inscribed in three rotating square the sides of each of which are decorated with four petals.

2 Hamsa/mayura with foliated tail, carrying a lotus flower in its beak. Eight-petalled lotus; plain vertical band; architectural facade constituted by a pair of split-pilasters with double capitals, compressed bevelled brackets, blocked-out doorway, high kapota, central kudu and foliage (?) design on top.

3 Architectural facade constituted by a pair of split-pilasters with double capitals, compressed bevelled brackets, doorway with shakas, high kapota and looped design (?) on top. Purnaghata decorated by a band at its centre, ending in two side tassels. In its opening is a coconut flanked by two stylized leaves falling along the neck of the pot. Architectural facade constituted by a pair of split-pilasters with double capitals, no brackets, kapota with central block, looped design (?) on top.

4 Purnaghata similar to the one in 3. In this example, however, the foliage sprouts from the coconut inserted into the opening of the vase, and the decorative band around its middle is more decorated. Architectural facade (torana) constituted by a pair of full pilasters, compressed bevelled brackets and multi-lobed frame composed of tassels with triple pendant buds. Circular creeper motif inscribed in a square.

5 Two concentric lotus motifs: a six-petalled flower in the inner circle and a 12-petalled flower in the outer circle. Architectural facade (torana) constituted by full pilasters with well articulated adhishthana footing blocks, double capitals and arched torana composed of garlands and a central medallion. Two concentric lotus motifs: an eight-petalled flower in the inner and outer circles.

6 Two concentric lotus motifs: an eight-petalled flower in the inner circle and a 14-petalled flower in the outer circle. Architectural facade constituted by a pair of split-pilasters with double capitals, bevelled brackets, doorway with single shakha, and kapota with blocked-out kudus. It is not clear what is at the top of the facade. Lotus motif: seven-petalled flower inscribed in a circle.

7 Two concentric lotus motifs: a 10-petalled flower in the inner circle and a 20-petalled flower in the outer circle. Architectural facade constituted by a pair of spilt pilasters with double capitals, brackets (?), a blocked-out doorway and kapota. Two concentric lotus motifs: an eight-petalled flower in the inner circle and a 16-petalled flower in the outer circle.

8 Two concentric lotus motifs: an eight-petalled lotus in the inner circle and a 10-petalled lotus in the outer circle. Architectural facade constituted by a pair of split-pilasters with double capitals, brackets (?), blocked out doorway (central portion damaged), recessed kantha with bands and kapota. Very faded hamsa/mayura.

9 Two concentric lotus motifs: a 12-petalled flower in the inner circle; the outer circle is worn. Architectural facade (partly concealed and damaged) constituted by a pair of pilasters and a blocked-out doorway.

WEST FACE

Gala (Course 6)

1 to **3** Blank.

4.99 An atlas-like figure part obscured by Phase IV.

NORTH FACE

Lower Upana (Course 2)

2.1 Nine panels are defined by plain bands and pilaster motifs. Each of the first four panels depict an left-facing elephant; the fifth panel shows a dance performance involving a dancer and two female mridanga-players similar to the scene on the east face (lower upana 2.6); the elephant motif is resumed in the next three panels. The last panel shows a wrestling match. One of the wrestlers performs an acrobatic feat by knotting his legs around the neck of his opponent. *(Plate 64)*

2.2 Eight unequal panels are defined by plain bands and pilaster motifs. Each of the first three panels shows a left-facing elephant. The fourth panel has a horseman with upraised right hand. In the fifth panel is an unfinished female figure with raised left hand. The sixth panel depicts a left-facing elephant. In the seventh panel are two elephants: the one plunges its trunk into the diminutive crown of a tree; the other proceeds towards a pillar, possibly suggesting a mansion. The last panel is occupied by a Central Asian chowkidar wearing a pointed cap, resting his left elbow on a staff. The figure is depicted frontally.

2.3 An elephant plunges the trunk in the crown of a tree, and another walks towards east.

2.4 Nine panels are defined by vertical bands and pilaster motifs. The first two panels show an elephant uprooting shrubs and an elephant moving towards the left. In the third panel, a groom armed with a staff curbs the last mentioned animal. Near the groom is a diminutive, damaged figure, possibly another groom. The fourth panel depicts a left-facing elephant uprooting a shrub. In the fifth panel a horseman rides a rearing animal, brandishing a sword in his right hand. The sixth panel accommodates a left-facing elephant. In the seventh panel a turbaned groom leads a horse by the bridle. In the eighth panel is a left-facing elephant. A man talks to a drummer in the last, ninth panel.

2.5 Eight and half panels are defined by plain bands and pilaster motifs. The sequence opens with a left-facing elephant. The second panel, divided into two parts, depicts a groom leading a horse by the bridle and, separated by the former by a pilaster, a female figure carrying an unidentified object in the left hand. Left-facing elephants occupy the third and the fourth panels. A huntress leaning on her bow is in the fifth panel, and a left-facing elephant in the sixth panel. The seventh panel has a Central Asian dancer. Finally, in the eighth panel there is yet another left-facing elephant. A faint carving showing the rump of an elephant concludes the block.

2.6 Seven and a half panels are defined by plain bands and pilaster motifs. The remaining part of the elephant noted in 2.5 begins the sequence of carvings. This is followed by two panels each with a left-facing elephant. One of the animals uproots shrubs, the other is shown pacing. The third panel shows an elephant led by a groom. The fourth panel has a dance scene with a female performer accompanied by female musicians playing the mridanga and cymbals. (This scene is similar to that on the east face, lower upana 2.6 and on the north face, lower upana 2.1.) The last three panels depict a horse and two elephants, the last of which, uproots shrubs.

2.7 This short panel (the north side of 2.1 on the east face) depicts an eight-petalled flower.

Gala (Course 6)

1 Vertical band (?). Two concentric lotus motifs: eight-petalled flower in the inner circle, and 16-petalled flower in the outer circle. Architectural facade: pair of split-pilasters with double capitals, bevelled brackets, doorway with petalled lintel, central block containing a 24-petalled lotus, and kapota with triple kudus. Two concentric lotus motifs: six-petalled flower in the inner circle and 36(?)-petalled flower in the outer circle.

2 Purnaghata with a coconut and foliage sprouting from its mouth, and a band with tassels in the middle. Architectural facade: pair of split-pilasters with double capitals (?), brackets, doorway with shakas and lintel block. Relief of hamsa/mayura in doorway. Kapota with five kudus (worn) and four finials. On a square set off from the wall, hamsa/mayura preening its plumage.

3 12-petalled lotus motif. Architectural facade: pair of split-pilasters (?) and brackets, upward-curved moulding and kapota with triple pot-like motifs (?). 12-petalled lotus motif.

4 On a square set off from the wall: hamsa/mayura. Purnaghata with coconut in foliage issuing from its mouth, and band and tassels around its middle. A 14-petalled lotus motif on a square set off from the wall.

5 Two concentric lotus motifs: an eight-petalled flower in the inner circle, and 16-petalled flower in the outer circle. Architectural facade: pair of split-pilasters with double capitals, bevelled brackets, blocked-out doorway, kapota with blocked-out central sections, and double recessed kanthas with bands separated by a moulding. Hamsa/mayura in a square frame.

6 Two concentric lotus motifs: a six-petalled flower in the inner circle, and 12-petalled flower in the outer circle. Architectural facade: pair of split-pilasters with double capitals (?), brackets, fanciful foliation on lintel and central petal-like design. Hamsa/mayura with a lotus stalk in its beak in a square frame.

7 Purnaghata with coconut and foliage issuing from the mouth of the vase. The band around its centre has tassels on either side. Architectural facade: pair of split-pilasters with double capitals (?), rolled brackets, blocked-out doorway and kapota with central kudu (?) topped by a reduced moulding. Hamsa/mayura with a lotus stalk in its beak (worn).

8 Two concentric lotus motifs: an eight-petalled flower in the inner circle, and eight-petalled flower in the outer circle. Architectural facade: pair of split-pilasters with double capitals, bevelled brackets, blocked-out doorway, kapota, two recessed kanthas (bands in the upper kanthas) and shala with central, arch-like window and triple kalasha finials. Two concentric lotus motifs: an eight-petalled flower in the inner circle, and 16-petalled flower in the outer circle.

9 Architectural facade: pair of spilt pilasters with double capital (?), brackets, blocked-out doorway, kapota, two recessed kanthas and shala with central, arch-like window and triple kalasha finials, all worn. Purnaghata with coconut and foliage issuing from its mouth and the usual decorative band at the centre with tassels on either side.

EAST FACE

Lower Upana (Course 2)

2.1 Nine panels separated by pillar motifs and plain vertical bands. The first five scenes are of elephants, of which the first, although shown proceeding towards the left, turns its head to face the viewer; the second animal, facing to the left, wraps its trunk around a tree; the next three elephants move towards the left. A woman carrying an arati tray is depicted in the sixth panel. The tray on which the five lamps are placed is carved onto the plain band separating this scene from the next. The seventh panel is occupied by a left-facing elephant uprooting a shrub. The eighth scene has a horseman brandishing a spear. A left-facing elephant concludes the series.

2.2 Nine panels divided by plain bands, of which one is unfinished. The first four panels show elephants: two elephants pace towards to the left, and two uproot shrubs. In the fifth panel is a long-cloaked, Central Asian groom leading a horse by the bridle. The theme of the elephants uprooting shrubs is resumed in the next two panels. The eighth panel is uncarved. The elephant on the ninth panel has not been completed.

2.3 Blank.

2.4 Partly obscured by the refurbished staircase leading to the Entrance Chamber, are two unfinished scenes. They depict a right-facing elephant, and a Central Asian dancer performing to the beat of a tambourine-player. *(Plate 65)*

2.5 Nine panels are defined by unsculpted bands. Each panel depicts a left-facing elephant. All of the elephants uproot shrubs with the exception of the first and third animals from the left; they are shown uplifting their trunk or walking respectively.

2.6 Eight panels defined by plain bands and pillar motifs. The first three panels from the right show left-facing elephants uprooting shrubs. In the fourth panel, a right-facing figure on a prancing horse carries a sword resting on his right shoulder. In the fifth panel is an elephant progressing towards the left. A dance performance involving a dancer (now damaged) and two female musicians playing the mridanga and cymbals is carved on to the sixth panel. In the seventh panel a huntress leans on her tall bow. In the eighth and final panel a horseman rests his sword on the left shoulder. *(Plate 66)*

2.7 South-facing hamsa.

Gala (Course 6)

1 Purnaghata with coconut and exuberant foliage issuing from the mouth of the vase. There is a ribbon around its central part and a tassel on the left. (The tassel on the right is now lost.) Architectural facade: pair of spilt pilasters with double capitals, pushpapodigai brackets, framing medallion and fanciful foliation symmetrically arranged on either side of a central tuft. At the centre of the facade is a lightly carved, 20-petalled lotus medallion. A hamsa/mayura with foliated tail and carrying a lotus stalk in its beak.

2 Lotus medallion with petals arranged in three concentric tiers of six petals each. Architectural facade: pair of split-pilasters with double capitals, pushpapodigai brackets, doorway with shakas and lintel block, and fanciful foliation symmetrically disposed either side of a central tuft. Two concentric lotus motifs: a 20-petalled flower in the inner circle, and 18-petalled flower in the outer circle.

3 Hamsa/mayura with foliated tail and lotus flower in its beak. Architectural facade: pair of split-pilasters with double capitals, rolled brackets, kapotas with kudus on either side of central blocked-out section and topmost, compressed moulding (?). Hamsa/mayura with foliated tail.

4 Eight-petalled lotus motif inscribed in a square set off from the wall. Four additional petals, flanked by two smaller petals, fill the corners of the square. Same type of architectural facade as in 3. Purnaghata with coconut and foliage motif issuing from the mouth of the vase, with band and tassels around its middle. All rather worn.

5 Purnaghata motif. The coconut has disappeared, but the foliage motif and other decoration have survived. Architectural facade: pair of split-pilasters with double capitals (?), kapota with triple kudus, recessed kantha with bands and kapota roof with kudus. Two concentric lotus motifs: a 12-petalled flower in the inner circle, and 24-petalled flower in the outer circle.

6 Plain band; eight-petalled lotus; plain band. Architectural facade: pair of pilasters with double capitals, rolled brackets, doorway with multiple shakas containing an eight-petalled lotus motif, and (worn) looped garlands on lintel. Plain band. Two concentric lotus motifs (worn): a six-petalled flower in the inner circle, and eight-petalled flower in the outer circle.

7 Pilaster; 14-petalled lotus motif; pilaster; 16-petalled lotus motif; pilaster; purnaghata, partly damaged.

8 Eight-petalled lotus motif (partly damaged); pilaster; purnaghata (worn); pilaster; hamsa/mayura carrying a lotus flower in its beak; four-petalled floral motif superimposed on a square;

vertical band; hamsa/mayura carrying a lotus flower in its beak.

9 Blank (?).

EAST ENTRANCE CHAMBER

Rear (West) Wall, First (Bottom) Row

These five male figures, depicting foreigners, are locally known and worshipped as the five Pandava brothers. All five figures are deeply carved. They are shown frontally and their feet rest on ledges.

The first figure from the right, perhaps a gate-keeper, wears a cap with a long streamer (?), a short lower garment set off by a broad long sash falling between the legs, and probably, a waist-length jacket with broad lapels. A short dagger is stuck among the folds of his sash. He sports a conspicuous moustache and triangular beard that accentuate his exotic features. He leans in a relaxed attitude, with slightly flexed knees, on the staff he carries in the right hand.

The second figure is a musician playing a tambourine. On his head is a tall conical ribbed cap; his ankle-length, lower garment is enlivened by a short pleated sash, and he wears a jacket. This figure, too, sports a similar type of moustache and beard as those already noted. Carried away by his own music, he is portrayed as if on the verge of starting to dance.

The third figure is a dancer wearing a pointed cap with a tassel (?) and upturned brim, decorated with a long streamer (due to the condition of the carving it is difficult to ascertain if this could be a pigtail). He is clad in a short lower garment and jacket. A pouch (?) hangs from the sash tied around his waist. The moustache and beard are the same as that already noted. He is rendered in an animated dance pose, and the slightly higher positioning on the wall makes this figure the most prominent of the lower row.

The fourth figure is another tambourine player wearing the same type of attire as the musician already described, and shown in the same stance.

The fifth figure, the last on the left, is a gate-keeper. He wears a pointed cap with a tassel, upturned brim, as noted above, and a thick pigtail. He sports the same moustache and beard as the other four men, and is clad in long, flowing robes. He is shown in a relaxed attitude resting his right elbow on a long staff. The left arm, also leaning on the staff, is placed at a striking angle to the body thus enhancing the rhythmic movement of the whole row. *(Plates 69, 70 and 71)*

Rear Wall, Second Row

Four male figures. As in the first row, these four men are of Central Asian origin. They are also deeply cut and shown frontally, each standing on a ledge. However, their movements are subdued, contrasting with the animated movements of the figures beneath.

The first figure is a gate-keeper. He wears the usual headgear, a thick pigtail and a long cloak. His triangular beard and moustache are prominently shown. His right hand rests on the long staff, while his left hand hangs at the side.

The second figure depicts a man wearing a conical ribbed cap, an ankle-length garment, and the usual moustache and beard. His left hand is placed on a staff, and in his right hand he carries a sword resting it on his shoulder.

The third figure, wearing an attire similar to the one just described, extends his left hand towards a cockerel (?). In his right hand he carries a sword, resting it on his shoulder.

The last and fourth figure in this row is that of a gate-keeper, wearing a conical cap with upturned brim, a pigtail, and a long, draped, lower garment. He leans with both hands on his staff. *(Plates 72 and 73)*

Rear Wall, Third Row

The three figure of this row are very unusual because they show Central Asians engaged in activities other than riding, fighting or parading horses. The first figure is a groom, armed with a forked staff, with which he tries to restrain an elephant rushing towards him. A large tree serves as backdrop. This scene is divided from the next by a tree inhabited by three monkeys. A hunter of Central Asian origins armed with spear and a shield effectively repels a tiger that leaps towards him from behind a tree. A third Central Asian figure carrying a pole across his shoulders is shown with flexed knees, suggesting a dancing pose. Finally, a right-facing elephant carrying a monkey (?) on its back wraps its trunk around the tree that divides this scene from the previous one. As in the rows beneath, the elephants and figures are shown standing on a ledge.

Rear Wall, Fourth (Top) Row

This consists of three framed panels. The first panel shows a large gatekeeper in the usual attire, resting his right hand and left foot on the staff. His gaze is directed towards a majestically pacing camel, on which sits a kettledrum player with a pointed conical cap adorned with a streamer. The animal is led by a diminutive groom, sporting a triangular tiered (?) cap (compare with the hats noted in Phase II, south face, 3.25 and 3.26). The groom moves in dance-like steps to the beat of the kettledrum.

The second panel is occupied by a large elephant uprooting shrubs, on which sit two local men dressed in knee-length garments. Their hair is tied in buns that rest on the napes of their necks.

The third panel mirrors the first: a large gatekeeper in typical attire, resting the right hand on his staff, carries an unidentified object in the raised left hand. He looks at a groom leading a camel on which sits a kettledrum-player similar to the one described above.

North Wall

A lower row of three panels separated by plain vertical bands. From right to left: The first scene shows a barely etched, unfinished rendering of a Central Asian gatekeeper. The second scene is devoted to a lively rendering of three Central Asian figures in the usual attire; two of them dance while playing on their instruments, the third dances using a scarf as a prop. In the third and last scene a reluctant horse is being tethered to a pole by a groom. The figure of the groom has now partly disappeared. The upper row consists of a single scene of a right-facing elephant uprooting a shrub, unfinished. *(Plate 67)*

South Wall

Three low relief panels separated by uncarved vertical bands. From left to right: Two gatekeepers are conversing; the one to the right, rests his right hand and left elbow on his staff. The remainder of the panel shows a Central Asian trader wearing a pointed cap and a long cloak, holding two horses by the bridle to either side. The second scene shows yet another gatekeeper carrying a staff in the right hand. The last scene, partly obscured, shows a standing figure. *(Plate 68)*

Staircases

North Staircase On the lower row on the left-hand wall are birds of various descriptions: two-headed bird pecking; hamsa in a medallion; peacock preening its plumage; and two-headed hamsa in a medallion. The only carving in the upper row depicts a hamsa. All the birds face left.

South Staircase On the lower row of the right-hand wall are carvings of a duck, peacock, two-headed peacock and duck pecking. On the upper row are two hamsas, one shown pecking. All the birds face right.

Access Steps The steps giving access to the East Entrance Chamber were only recently placed in the present position, the blocks having been removed from some other part of the monument (?). On the left face of the lowermost step is a fragment of a figure with the right arm raised, and a shallow carving of a fish. Resting on the top of the sixth row of Phase II are two blocks. That on the left has a creeper and hamsa/mayura motif on its left face. That on the right has a fragment of a Vasantotsava scene on its right-hand face. This shows five female dancers with a basin placed on the ground nearby.

Chapter Ten

CARVINGS OF PHASE IV

The projecting and returning segments of the chloritic schist mouldings on each of the bottom, middle and top series of mouldings on the west face of the platform are here given individual designations (see *Figure 9*).

BOTTOM SERIES

Jagati (Course 5), South Part

S-S1
1 to **3** Blank.
4 Fragment: caparisoned elephant facing left.
5 to **6** Blank.

S-W1
7 Blank
8 Three right-facing elephants. The first animal from the right wraps its trunk around of a tree; the second animal is damaged. (Possibly a misplaced block.)
9 Two caparisoned elephants facing left.

S-S2
10 to **12** Blank, except for the occasional letter/number in Tamil script (placed upside down).

S-W2
13 to **15** Blank.
16 Damaged block: four caparisoned elephants facing left.
17 Damaged block: three (?) elephants facing left. (The stone here seems different to the usual chloritic schist.)
18 Partly damaged. Three caparisoned elephants facing left. The central animal is restrained by a groom wearing a pointed cap with ear flaps. (This headdress seems to have been typical of elephant grooms in the 16th century.)
19 Three caparisoned elephants facing left.

Jagati (Course 5), North Part

N-N1
1 to **3** Blank.
4 Letter/number in Telugu script.

N-W1
5 Blank.
6 Three caparisoned elephants facing right. The central animal, facing left, places its trunk on the back of that to the left.
7 Five caparisoned elephants facing right. The second from right is shown uprooting shrubs.
8 Three caparisoned elephants facing right. The first animal from the left, looks backwards.
9 A groom wearing a kullayi and conspicuous earrings tethers a riotous elephant to a tree. The elephant turns its head towards its tail. Three elephants facing right complete the scene.
10 Three elephants facing right. The central animal pushes the one before it, while a groom counteracts the impact of the thrust by gripping it by its trunk.
11 Blank.

N-N2
12 Three caparisoned and decorated elephants facing right.
13 A right-facing elephant.

N-W2
14 Four elephants, two of which face to the right. The two animals in the middle face each other, their tusks crossed. A groom wearing a bulbous headgear, armed with an elephant goad, restrains the animal on the right by grabbing its tusks.

15 to **17** Blank.
18 A left-facing, lion-like animal. To the left are traces of a human figure (?). (This block may have been misplaced.)
19 A caparisoned elephant rushes towards a groom armed with a long forked staff. A second animal is restrained by another groom, who thrusts his staff in its trunk. A third elephant uproots a shrub. Both grooms are of athletic build. They wear short lower garments and their hair is tied in topknots.
20 A groom, dressed as in 19, restrains an elephant by hitting its trunk with a staff. Another elephant wraps its trunk around a tree.

Lower Gala (Course 6), South Part

S-S1
1-2 Blank.

S-W1
3 Blank.
4 Fragments of a misplaced block. The legs of two dancing girls wearing flared skirts. A basin, presumably for coloured water, is carved at either end of the scene, which might have belonged to a frieze of dancers and revellers of the Vasantotsava.
5 to **7** Blank, except for a letter/number in Tamil script.
8 Blank.

S-S2
9 to**12** Blank.

S-W2
13 Blank.
14 Damaged block, possibly misplaced. Legs of a male mridanga-player. Traces of another figure at the left-hand end of the block.
15 Blank.
16 A possibly misplaced block representing the Vasantotsava celebration. Two young women dance near a basin of water to be squirted in the course of the festivities. Both maidens are elegantly dressed. One wears a knee-length, lower garment tied like a dhoti and enlivened by a long pleated sash falling at the front. The other is dressed in a three-tiered skirt fastened at the waist by a long sash. Their long hair is tied in a topknots pinned slightly off-centre on the crowns of the heads. Both maidens carry cups, presumably for coloured water. The left-hand figure is remarkably well preserved.
17 Fragment of a battle scene. The right-hand portion of the scene was probably occupied by a horseman, followed by one or possibly two parasol-bearers. These figures have practically disappeared. The left-hand and central portions of the scene show remains of an army and a battle, with a warrior and dying man. Particularly striking are the small round shields held by the soldiers, which are decorated with conspicuous floral motifs. *(Plate 81)*
18 Fragment of a battle scene. At either end are troops carrying small round shields, as in 17. At the centre of the composition was a horseman, now completely obliterated. (It is possible that blocks 17 and 18 have been misplaced.) *(Plate 81)*
19 Two soldiers, armed with sword and round shield facing north. (This block is possibly misplaced.)
20 A left-facing horse. The rest of the block has been defaced.
21 From right to left: A man with a short lower garment, hair tied in a topknot, and a raised sword in his hand, leads a horse by its bridle. A second man wielding a long, S-shaped sword leads a second horse.
22 The focus of the action is seen on the left-hand portion of the scene. Here a horseman on a galloping horse tramples on a supine warrior armed with a large round shield. The right-hand portion is occupied by a groom, attired as in the figure in 21, leading a horse by the bridle.

Lower Gala (Course 6), North Part

N-N1
1 to **3** Blank.

N-W1
4 Blank
5 Three caparisoned, unsaddled horses facing to the right.
6 A groom, armed with a sword and a round shield, walks behind an elephant carrying his mahout. A rearing tiger attacks the elephant,

but is stabbed in the stomach by a warrior, standing opposite to the elephant. At the same time a courtly rider, arriving from the right on a prancing horse, plunges a spear into the neck of the tiger. The man wears a tall kullayi and a billowing scarf of honour on his left shoulder. The horseman is followed by a parasol-bearer and two retainers armed with curved swords and round shields. A third attendant stands near to the horse. *(Plate 80)*

7 Three caparisoned, unsaddled horses facing right. The tail of the horse to at the right is raised up.

8 A pacing horse led by a groom; a prancing horse with a raised, bushy tail; two pacing horses. All four horses are unsaddled and face to the right.

9 A prancing horse checked by a foreign groom clad in the typical long cloak; a cantering horse. The animals are unsaddled and face to the right.

10 A rearing unsaddled horse and a cantering horse, both with upright tails, proceed to the right.

11 An unsaddled horse is led by a turbaned groom, preceded by another groom. The figures face to the right. A tree delimits the scene to the left.

N-N2

12 Fragment of a horse; a pacing, unsaddled horse. Both animals face to the right.

13 A man wearing a bulbous headgear, armed with an S-shaped sword and round shield with a conspicuous floral motif (as in lower gala, south part, 17). The figure is preceded by two unsaddled facing horses facing right.

N-W2

14 A groom wearing a kullayi-like cap restrains an unsaddled galloping horse.

15 Three unsaddled horses facing right. A groom holds the central animal by the reins.

16 to **17** Blank.

18 A group of four dancing women. The two women to the left carry a large pot between them, while those to the right each hold a flask and cup. The women are splendidly dressed in full-length skirts decorated with girdles falling in loops of different length in front. They wear long scarves around their arms, and their hair is either gathered in long plaits, or in buns pinned at the side of their heads. (The block, of granite rather than chloritic schist, has been misplaced.)

19 Two grooms lead one horse each. The animal on the right portion of the block has been deeply cut. The animals face to the left. (The block, of granite rather than chloritic schist, has been misplaced.)

20 The left-hand portion of this block has disappeared. However, it is possible to make out vestiges of an unsaddled horse led by a foreign groom. The remainder of the scene shows three unsaddled horses. From right to left: the first horse is led by a groom (defaced); the second horse moves to the right; the third horse has its head turned towards the left.

Upper Gala (Course 8), North Part

N-N1

1 to **4** Blank.

N-W1

5 to **7** Blank

8 Three women dancing and preparing for the water squirting activities of the Vasantotsava festival. They are elegantly dressed: the first two women from the left wear tights and short skirts with pleated frilled sashes; the third woman wears a long skirt enhanced by a two-tiered, frilled sash. A large basin for coloured water is placed nearby, at the right-hand end of the block. The central figure carries a cup in her raised left hand.

9 The centre of the block is occupied by a courtly couple embracing in a structure defined by pillars and colonnettes. To the left are three women: one carries a fly-whisk; another a sword; a third an unidentified object. To the right, six further women attend on the couple. Each woman carries some item that might be required. All the women wear full length skirts, draped like a dhoti, fastened at the waist by multi-stringed girdles falling in loops of various lengths in front. Their attire is completed by long, billowing scarves carried around one of their arms. Their hair is fastened in buns at the sides of their heads. A narrow band with a

foliage scroll motif concludes the panel to the right. (It is possible that this panel has been misplaced.) *(Plate 82)*
10 Three women dancing. The one to the left, dressed in a two-tiered skirt, is flanked by two large basins for coloured water. The remaining two women are attired in long flaring skirts, with their hair tied in buns at the sides of their heads. They carry flasks in both hands.
11 Fragment: female figure (?).

N-N2
12 Blank.
13 Two male musicians wearing kullayis and long jackets play the trumpet and mridanga.
14 A figure with hands folded in anjali mudra stands opposite a tree. A creeper concludes the panel to the left. (Possibly this block has been misplaced.)

N-W2
15 Vertical band with a creeper motif. A woman sits on a low stool, beneath which is a pitcher. She gazes at her reflection in the mirror, while adjusting her hair tied in a bun on the crown of the head. (Possibly this block has been misplaced.)
16 Two dancers wearing tights and short, wide, flaring skirts. One dancer raises her right hand; the other her left hand, while resting her right hand on the thigh. *(Plate 83)*
17 A man, possibly an ascetic, with raised hands. The figure has lightly etched, long matted hair, a detail that seems to have been an afterthought. (Possibly this block has been misplaced.)
18 Fragment of a woman dancing, her billowing scarf draped in a loop around her shoulders. Originally there was another figure, of which only one hand carrying a flask remains.
19 Partly damaged. Three female dancers dressed in tights, short skirts enhanced by decorated looped girdles and long scarves. The two figures to the left each carry each a cup in one hand. The third figure is badly damaged. (Possibly this block has been misplaced.)
20 Three female dancers dressed in tights and short skirts with elaborate, frilled sashes around their waists. (Possibly this block has been misplaced.)
21 to **25** Blank.

MIDDLE SERIES

Lower Upana (Course 1), South Part

S-SE
Fragments of a dance scene (left) and a figure seated near a tree (right).

S-W1
1-2 Blank.
3 Damaged: two left-facing elephants.
4 Blank.
5 A left-facing elephant.
6 Four caparisoned elephants facing left.
7 Five caparisoned elephants facing left. The first elephant from the right wraps its trunk around a tree.
8 Five caparisoned elephants facing left. A tree separates the left-hand elephant from the other animals.
9 A groom dressed in a short lower garment and wearing a tall cap with ear-flaps supervises with the help of a forked staff an elephant uprooting shrubs. A tree separates this scene from the next, in which two elephants are each uprooting a tree. To the left is a similarly dressed groom carrying a forked staff.

S-S2
10 A caparisoned elephant facing left.
11 Five caparisoned elephants, four of which face left. The fifth elephant faces right and crosses tusks with the fourth left-facing one.
12 From right to left: An elephant uproots a tree to which a second elephant is chained. In turn, it wraps its trunk around the tree to which the third animal is tethered. All the animals face to the left.

S-W2
13 A caparisoned elephant, facing left, wraps its trunk around a tree.
14 Two left-facing elephants. At either end of the scene is a tree.
15 An elephant and a groom with raised arm, as if ready to strike the animal's forehead. A second elephant is shown pacing. A third elephant seizes a groom by the waist, witnessed

by two courtly figures wearing kullayis, one of whom raises his right hand. A fourth elephant grabs the arm and lower garment of its groom. The last scene shows a fifth elephant running to the left. *(Plate 85)*
16 Two pairs of elephants confronting each other. The pair to the right, richly caparisoned and wearing elaborate head-cloths, run towards each other. A tree separates them from the pair to the left, which are shown crossing their tusks. A tree to the left completes the scene.

Lower Upana (Course 1), North Part

N-W1
1 To the left, a groom in the usual attire stands near a forked pole, looking at three elephants moving to the right.
2 Four caparisoned elephants facing right.
3 Four caparisoned elephants facing right.
4 To the left a groom holds an unidentified object in the raised right hand; three caparisoned elephants move to the right.
5 Four elephants facing left. The first and the last animals wrap their trunks around trees. (Possibly this block has been misplaced.)
6 A tree and a right-facing elephant. (The block, of granite rather than choloritic schist, has been misplaced.)
7 A tree and four caparisoned elephants facing to the right.
8 A south-facing elephant. (The block, of granite rather than choloritic schist, has been misplaced.)

N-N2
9 A right-facing caparisoned elephant.
10 A caparisoned elephant grabs a groom by the waist and hurls him head first to the ground. Another elephant rushes towards a second groom, who runs away brandishing a forked staff. A tree to the right concludes the scene. (The block, of granite rather than choloritic schist, has been misplaced.)
11 An elephant tramples on a groom who has fallen to the ground. A second groom tries to curb the mad animal by prodding a staff into its hind parts. A third groom sticks a fork into the animal's forehead. Two right-facing elephants conclude the scene. *(Plate 84)*
12 A right-facing elephant.

N-W2
13 A group of four elephants proceeds to the right. They are preceded by a groom wearing a kullayi and wielding a staff.
14 Two right-facing elephants.
15 Two right-facing elephants, and the hind part of a third elephant.
16 The head of the elephant in 15, and another elephant, both facing right.
17 Four right-facing elephants. The animal at the right end of the block is damaged.

Gala (Course 5) and Niche Projections, South Part

S-W1
1 to **4** Blank.
5 A girl dressed in a triple-tiered, flared skirt held at the waist by a pleated sash dances carries a cup in her raised right hand. A basin for coloured water is placed on the ground nearby. A fruit tree concludes the scene to the left. (This is probably a misplaced block.)
6 Two dancing girls perform with gusto. They wear tights and short skirt, and their hair is gathered into conspicuous bouffants at the crowns of their heads. A vertical band with creeper design completes the scene to the right.
Niche S1 A standing male figure wearing a loose lower garment, jacket and kullayi. He is flanked by two richly attired females.
7 A dancing girl performs while a male musician punctuates the rhythm of the dance with his cymbals. The left-hand portion of the scene is occupied by two female musicians with vina and mridanga. Two vertical bands with foliage designs complete the scene to the left.
8 Two dancing girls performing. They are dressed in tights and short skirts enlivened by girdles falling in decorative loops at the front. Their hair is gathered in topknots pinned slightly to one side of their heads. They are separated by a vertical band with foliage design.
Niche S2 Standing male dressed in courtly attire.
9 The focus of the composition is a courtly figure seated on a low asana receiving four noblemen. The courtly figure wears a knee-

length, lower garment, a yajnopavita on his bare chest, and the usual jewellery, including a pendeya on his right foot, a scarf of honour on his left shoulder and a kullayi. Behind him are three female attendants clad in full-length, lower garments draped like a dhoti, enhanced by girdles decorated with triple loops. They carry a chauri, pouch and sword respectively. The costumes of the four noblemen are simpler, though they wear conspicuous sashes wrapped around their waists. *(Plate 90)*

10 A vertical band with foliage motif separates the two scenes. To the right is a male dancer carrying a cup in his raised left hand. He is flanked by two dancing girls attired in the usual tights and short, two-tiered skirts holding goblets in one their hands. To the left are two dancing girls, one with a flask and goblet in the hands, the other with a goblet only. A broad uncarved band defines the lower part of the block.

11 Blank.

S-S2

12 Three standing male figures wearing kullayis pay homage to a courtly personage, who is also shown standing. All the figures wear jackets and what seem to be loose trousers. The waists of the three visitors are set off by broad sashes covering the hips. The courtly personage wears the scarf of honour draped on his left shoulder. *(Plate 89)*

13 Defaced. A dancing girl next to a water basin placed on the ground.

Gala (Course 5) and Niche Projections, North Part

N-W1

1 A woman (facing to the right) picks up something from the ground. A basin for coloured water is placed nearby. Two women, each holding a flask, stand on either side of a shallow basin. The women all wear long flared skirts. (Possibly this block has been misplaced.)

2 Two vertical bands with foliage designs separate the scenes. To the left are two dancing girls wearing leggings and short skirts, their hair gathered in conspicuous knots at the sides of their heads. In the middle are three, similarly attired dancers. To the right are a quartet of musicians: three males play cymbals, mridanga and nagasvaram; a woman carries a vina on her shoulder. *(Plate 86)*

Niche N1 Only three damaged figures survive. The principal figure, probably a female judging from the vestiges of the hairstyle, has totally disappeared. This was flanked by a male to the left and female to the right. Further right is a chowkidar (?) leaning on a staff. He wears a conspicuous headgear. *(Plate 86)*

3 The two scenes are separated by a vertical band with foliage motifs. The carving to the left shows a tree and dancing girl; another dancing girl is seen to the right.

4 Two dancing girls in the usual attire.

Niche N2 The central figure has disappeared. Figure at either side survive, though damaged; a chowkidar to the left, and male attendant to the right. Their strikingly individual features suggest that they may portray specific persons.

5 Three scenes separated by a vertical band with foliage designs. The sequence opens to the left with a dancing girl dressed in tights and a short skirt with a frilled edge. In the middle there is a dancing mistress in a long dhoti-like lower garment. Her majestic stance and imperious hand movement suggest that she is conducting the performance. She is flanked by two dancing girls dressed in skirts of various types and lengths. To the right is a male tambourine-player. (This figure is similar to, but more elongated and leaner than, those on other parts on the monument.) He wears a conspicuous girdle (?) constituted by leaf-shaped elements, jacket and cap. A scarf is fastened onto his jacket. He is flanked by two dancing girls in the usual attire. *(Plates 87 and 88)*

6 Two scenes separated by a vertical band with foliage design. To the left is a dancing girl carrying a cup (?) in her raised hand. Two dancing girls, carrying similar objects in their hands, are seen to the right.

W-N2

7 A woman carrying a staff sits on a left-facing makara.

8 Two scenes separated by a vertical band with foliage design, with similar bands at either end of the block. To the left, a man with a cup in

his hand is flanked by two dancing girls, both carrying goblets. A basin for water is placed on the ground nearby. To the right, three dancing girls celebrating. Two basins rest on the ground in between the dancers. The dancer to the right of the first one seems be an afterthought.
9 Blank.

TOP SERIES

Gala (Courses 5 and 6) and Niche Projections, South Part

S-W1
Niche S1 Female figure clutching a creeper with the left hand; her right arm is raised.
Kumbhapanjara flanked by two female figures. The figure to the right gracefully raises her right hand. The figure to the left, elegantly standing with crossed feet, embraces a creeper which surrounds her completely.
Niche S2 A woman stands under a lobed arch. Her left hand rests on her thigh; her right hand is raised to her face.
Niche S3 A male figure wearing a kullayi, with the scarf of honour draped on his left shoulder, is seated in the typical pose of the royal figure. (Probably this block has been haphazardly inserted.)

S-S2
A woman stands between two pilasters in a graceful pose, similar to that beneath niche S2.

S-W3
Niche S4 Missing.
Kumbhapanjara To the right stands an elegantly posed woman looking to the south. Her right hand, however, points to the kumbhapanjara.

Gala (Courses 5 and 6) and Niche Projections, North Part

N-W2
Kumbhapanjara To the left, a chowkidar carrying a long staff. He wears a bulbous headgear similar to that worn by a figure in the middle series, gala, N1. To the right, a female figure bending her right leg so as to touch with her foot the foliage sprouting from the pot. *(Plates 92 and 94)*
Niche N1 Male courtly figure, partly destroyed. To the left, a female attendant; to the right, an amorous couple. Dressed in sumptuous courtly attire, complete with kullayi and scarf, the male delicately lifts the chin of his female companion. *(Plates 92 and 93)*
Niches N2 to **N4** Missing.

N-W3
Kumbhapanjara Two lions leap out from the foliage sprouting from the vase.

West Staircase

Fully carved, though damaged, sculptures of two pacing elephants flank the bottom steps of the staircase. (They were placed here during the reconstruction of the monument.)

Missing Block

During conservation work in the 20th century some blocks of Phase IV were left lying about. A number of these are still stacked near to the north enclosure wall, but others have been lost. One of the missing blocks, of particular artistic interest, was published when still in situ, though unfortunately it is not possible from the photograph to determine its precise location (Longhurst 1925 [1917]: 65). The block depicts a Vasantotsava scene, with an embracing couple dancing. Both figures raise a cup of coloured water, the man in the left hand and the women in the right hand. The couple is accompanied by three maidens, two carrying squirts and a third a cup. The male figure wears a kullayi. The three women are dressed in tights and short skirts; their hair is gathered in bouffants at the top of their heads. (*Figure 13*; p. 158)

Appendix I

FESTIVALS

Although it cannot be definitively ascertained that the Great Platform played a central role in the annual Mahanavami celebrations at Vijayanagara, and although the sculpted friezes do not appear to have any direct or indirect connection to this festival, it remains in the popular imagination and tradition that the monument has been in some way associated with this event. Therefore it useful to have a brief account of the mythological background and ritual role of the king during the celebrations of the Mahanavami/Dasara, especially since this festival has continued to be the epitome of royal power in the post-Vijayanagara period, up to the present day, with the sumptuous annual celebrations that take place in Mysore.

NAVARATRI, MAHANAVAMI AND VIJAYADASHAMI

According ritual treatises and early mythology, there are two festivals called Navaratri Nine Nights. The first, celebrated roughly at the time of the spring equinox, during the bright half of the month of Chaitra (April-May), marks the beginning of the lunar year. It was possibly an agrarian festival in which the goddesses were worshipped to ensure regeneration and abundance of plant and animal life. During the Vijayanagara period this was the time of the Spring festival, or Vasantotsava. Today, however, this association appears to have been forgotten and, instead, the focus of the festivities is Rama's birth. The second Navaratri festival, roughly coincides with the autumn equinox, and commemorates Durga's victory over Mahishasura. It begins on the first and ends on the ninth day, Mahanavami, i.e. the Great Ninth, of the bright fortnight of the month of Ashvina, or Ashvayuja, which corresponds to the lunar months of September-October. Numerous religious ceremonies take place during this period. In many localities a tenth day, called Vijayadashami, Victorious Tenth, is added, hence the name of Dasara, Tenth Day. This day commemorates Rama's victory over Ravana, or, according to another tradition, the end of the Mahabharata war.

The mythological background which forms the basis of this festival is the well-known myth of Durga's victory over Mahishasura, as narrated in the *Devi-Mahatmya*, a Sanskrit work probably composed during the 8th century, embedded in the *Markandeya Purana*. The myth of Durga's victory over Mahishasura, thus redressing the balance between good and evil, was an inspiration for many kings and feudal rulers to propitiate her for success in their military expeditions. Indian literature is replete with legends of heroes seeking her blessings, e.g. in the Virata-parvan section of the *Mahabharata,* Yudhishthira, the eldest of the Pandava princes, worships Durga before entering the capital of king Virata, where he together with his four brothers and their common wife Draupadi will spend the last year of exile in disguise. In his eulogy, Yudhishthira invokes the goddess by her many epithets: 'slayer of the buffalo-demon', 'the one who loves intoxicating drinks, flesh and animal sacrifices', Kali, and 'the one who dwells on the Vindhya mountains'. The prince prays for protection from danger, sickness and death. The goddess, pleased with his prayers, assures him victory in battle. The other famous hero, who seeks the help of the goddess in winning a war, is Rama. Although this episode does not appear in Valmiki's *Ramayana,* it is incorporated in many later versions of the story, beginning from the 6th century *Devi Bhagavata Purana* (III, 30). One of the most famous versions of this incident is narrated in the 15th century Bengali *Ramayana* by Krittivasa. All these narratives relate how a despondent Rama is at a loss on how to win the battle against Ravana and rescue Sita. Narada, the divine seer, encourages him to invoke the goddess Durga, advising him on the correct performance of the ritual. To demonstrate the efficacy of this ritual, Narada tells Rama that many divine personalities have worshipped Durga before venturing into crucial conflicts: Shiva, prior to fighting the Tripurasuras, Vishnu before slaying Madhu and Kaitabha, and Indra before annihilating Vritra. While Rama is completing the puja, the goddess mounted on her lion appears before him and grants him victory (Kinsley 1996: 109).

Historical rulers also worshipped Durga for success in military expeditions, however, only after the Gupta epoch in north India and at the end of the Chola period in the south, her cult developed into a splendid ten-day festival. Burton Stein very perceptively suggests the reasons why the Navaratri and Vijayadashami festivals became such a major event at a relatively late period in Indian history. He observes that the Gupta kings celebrated extremely elaborate and costly rites such as the ashvamedha, horse sacrifice, the rajasuya, royal consecration, and the vajapeya, drink of power, and thus, they had no need of a separate war festival. The kings of the early period were deemed to partake of the essential energy of Vishnu's character, and thus did not require to ask for blessings. What was necessary for them was to replenish their divine powers through rituals and to link them to the cosmic order. However, according to Stein, by the end of the Gupta period, 'kings were divested of the sacred stuff they were deemed to possess, partly ascriptively, by birth as kshatriyas, and partly by the contingent outcome of their periodic ritual regeneration; there was even a prohibition of those great royal sacrifices whose object was to infuse kings with divine power.... What divine qualities were lost to individual kings, however, appear to have been gained by the institution of kingship' (Stein 1983: 303-5). Thus, the sanctity of kingship became the paramount preoccupation. The cult of the warrior goddess who blessed the symbols of kingship: the throne, the sword, the crown, the army, etc. and sanctioned the king's authority to reign for another year, replaced the elaborate Vedic rituals celebrating individual kings.

In order to stress the idea of kingship 'as a sacred condition', public rituals such as the Mahanavami were necessary (Stein 1983: 311). The festival seems to have come into existence, or at least the first reports of it, date of the Vijayanagara period. It is at this point in time, that new, martial elements, such as worship of weapons, chariots, and royal insignias, were added to the original goddess cult. Furthermore, all animals used in war were honoured: elephants, horses and camels, and animal sacrifices were made to Durga to stimulate her martial spirit and vengeful violence. All kingly appurtenances, such as the throne, crown and sword, were identified with Durga. Myths were created, narrating how a special weapon was given to the king by the family goddess, to conquer and vanquish the enemy. One example is the famous episode of the 17th century Maratha leader Shivaji, who received his sword from the hand of his tutelary goddess, Bhavani. It bore the name Bhavani, and was always with him; when not in use it was placed on the goddess's altar where it was worshipped on every Navaratri festival. On Dasara day, just before starting on a new expedition, the goddess was deemed to return it to him with her blessings (Kinsley 1996: 109-10). The timing of the festival, at the end of the monsoon season, when the sky is clear, the rivers fordable, and the harvest provides plenty of food for the troops, may have played a role: once the festival had come to an end, it would have been the ideal time for the ruler, empowered by the blessing of the goddess, to set out on military campaigns.

Navaratri and Vijayadashami are associated not only with the ancient worship of Durga, but also with the much more recent tradition of Rama's victory over Ravana, which is celebrated on Vijayadashami day. Both these traditions lie at the basis of the Dasara celebrations in various parts of India. In the north Indian Hindi-speaking belt, Rama's victory is commemorated with great eclat. In eastern and southern India the worship of Durga holds centre stage, whereas in regions such as Gujarat and Maharashtra both traditions are celebrated.

FROM VIJAYANAGARA'S MAHANAVAMI TO MYSORE'S ROYAL DASARA

Imitating the pomp and circumstance of the Vijayanagara rayas, the local rulers of the successor states celebrated the Mahanavami festival to demonstrate their own power and wealth to their subjects. They adopted all the major features of the Mahanavami celebrations, as established during the time of the Vijayanagara Rayas, and the festival continued to be celebrated with great solemnity and splendour in various capitals of the successor states.

Mysore emerged as an independent state under the rule of Raja Wodiyar (1578-1617).[1] Srirangapattana, had been for nearly two centuries under the sway of the Vijayanagara rayas. It now became the seat of the Mysore rulers. Raja Wodiyar moved his capital from Mysore to Srirangapattana on 21 March 1610. Venkata II of the Aravidu dynasty unable to reconquer the lost territory finally recognized him independent ruler of Srirangapattana and Ummattur in 1612. As an independent ruler, Raja Wodiyar was the true inheritor of the Vijayanagara cultural traditions. He celebrated the Mahanavami and Vijayadashami festivals on a grand scale, worthy of the Vijayanagara rayas, from 8 to 17 September in the same year. This custom was observed by all subsequent kings of the Wodiyar dynasty.

Although there is no verifiable proof that the celebrations continued during the thirty eight years of the rule of Haidar Ali and Tipu Sultan, it is probable that the festival took place regularly until at least 1796 when Khasa Chamaraja died, and Tipu Sultan ignored the claims of his successor. After the death of Tipu Sultan on 4 May 1799, Marquess Wellesley gave a portion of Tipu Sultan's territory to the descendants of the Wodiyar dynasty. On 30 June of that year, the five year old Nanjaraja ascended the throne as Krishnaraja Wodiyar III (Mummadi Krishnaraja). As the king was still a young child, the state administration was in the hands of Divan Purnaiya and the British Resident. The capital was moved from Srirangapattana to Mysore, and, in the autumn of 1800, the festival was celebrated there for the first time, where it continues to this day, albeit on a reduced scale.

VASANTOTSAVA

There was, however, another significant festival, which took place roughly six months before the Mahanavami. This was the spring festival, which focuses on the worship of Kamadeva, also called Vasanta (spring), the god of love. Its mythological background is based on a famous incident: the burning of Kamadeva. Local tradition has placed this myth in a clearly defined spatial setting. The main characters are Pampa, possibly an ancient river goddess, who became the tutelary goddess of Hampi, and Virupaksha, an aspect of Shiva. In the pre-Vijayanagara period, the goddess was 'Sanskritized' through her marriage to Virupaksha, and she became Pampambika, one of the forms of Parvati. To become Shiva's wife, Pampa had to undergo severe austerities, not, as usual, on the Himalayas, but at Pampasaras near Hampi, while Shiva was deep in meditation on nearby Hemakuta hill. The gods, anxious to arrange the wedding of Shiva and Pampa, sent Kamadeva armed with his arrows to distract Shiva from meditation, and throw a brief glance on Pampa. Shiva retaliated by incinerating him with his blazing third eye. Rati, Kamadeva's wife, was inconsolable. Shiva, moved by her grief, relented and agreed that once a year Kama would resume his bodily form. On this day the Vasantotsava is celebrated.

The spring festival at Vijayanagara has been described in numerous literary sources both in Sanskrit and in Kannada. One of the most relevant Sanskrit works is Ahobala's *Virupaksha Vasantotsava Champu*, an elaborate 15th-century poem containing a detailed description of the Vasantotsava and the festival of Virupaksha that took place at Hampi.[2] Two elements were combined in this celebration: the wedding of Virupaksha and Pampambika, and the

Vasantotsava. Both events called for merriment, music, dance and general rejoicing.

This festival lasted nine days, commencing with the ceremonial flag hoisting in the Virupaksha temple on the ninth day of the bright fortnight of Chaitra (April-May). The rathotsava, or car-festival, took place on the full moon day. On this occasion, the king was expected to take an active part in the proceedings and join those in charge of pulling the chariot. Without the presence and participation of the ruler, the chariot could not be moved. This point is particularly important because the king becomes both a devotee, who must take part in the physical act of pulling the chariot containing the divine image, and simultaneously he is 'divine himself, inasmuch as the car will not move without the agency of the ruler' (Krishna Das 1996: 212).

The *Virupaksha Vasantotsava Champu* describes the figures of Kamadeva and his retinue placed prominently on the temple chariot. Saffron coloured water was thrown on the assembled crowds. This latter feature survives in the present-day chariot festival of the Virupaksha temple, although instead of saffron-water, coloured powder is thrown on the participants.[3]

The rathotsava was followed by the Mrigayotsava, the hunting festival, when the god was taken out on a hunting expedition on the far side of the river. This again stresses the parallel between the king and the deity. According to Anderson (1993: 189-90): 'As a hunter, particularly in the midst of the city of Vijayanagara, the deity is figuratively identified with the king whose fondness for such sports is [renowned]. Virupaksha's foray into the forest becomes both a royal as well as a divine expedition as the actions and demeanour of Virupaksha (Shiva) are in consonance with those of the king. Both extend their influence beyond the banks of the Tungabhadra and into the untamed forest region: Virupaksa by identifying the wooden territories as the abode of the same deity who resides in the temple (Shiva); the king who, by extension, identifies the forest as royal domain, as the hunting ground of the king.'

In the forest Virupaksha met a number of 'forest ladies', and this excited the goddess' jealousy: this part of the story is also highlighted in the festival. The couple were reconciled, and finally the kalyanotsava, wedding, took place. This festival has been celebrated more or less without interruption until the present day and its modern 'version' displays many similarities with the one described by Ahobala.[4]

Judging by the sculptures, the artists' attention was concentrated on the Vasantotsava rather than on the wedding of Virupaksha and Pampambika. Depictions of Kama, his consort Rati and their retinue, all riding on chariots drawn by parrots and swans, throwing flower tipped arrows or flowers at each with great gusto, occur on various monuments of the city along with the ubiquitous revellers dancing, squirting water at each other and, occasionally, embracing.[5]

NOTES

1. In a mere 30 years, from being a mere chief of 33 villages, chief of 300 soldiers and with a modest revenue, Raja Wodiyar became ruler of a sizeable kingdom. This was the cause of a strife with the Vijayanagara Viceroy at Srirangapattana, Tirumalaraya II, a nephew of the Aravidu king Venkata II (1568-1614), who ruled what was left of the Vijayanagara empire from Penukonda. Disagreements between the uncle and the nephew gave an opportunity to Raja Wodiyar to attack Srirangapattana. The Viceroy handed over the kingdom and the royal throne to Raja Wodiyar and then retired to a small village, Malingi, south-east of Mysore.
2. For a detailed analysis and interpretation of this work see Anderson (1993: 171-97).
3. Panchamukhi (1953: xii).
4. Krishna Das (2006: 319-37).
5. A particularly fine set of carvings illustrating this episode is on the south face of the basement of the stone chariot in the Vitthala temple.

Appendix II

CENTRAL ASIANS AND OTHER FOREIGNERS

One of the most striking features of the carvings on the Great Platform is the conspicuous presence of foreigners. Judging from their appearance in the carvings some were traders, others were employed in the royal household as master of ceremonies or doorkeepers; some were courtly entertainers; the majority, however, were soldiers who enrolled mainly in the cavalry. The decimation of the Vijayanagara army during the constant troubles with the Bahmani sultans persuaded Devaraya II (1424-46) to reform the structure of the armed forces and to create a stgrong cavalry and corps of archers enrolling Muslims.

Recent scholarship, however, reveals that, "even prior to this period [i.e. Devaraya's reforms] there was a significant Muslim presence at court in the form of Central Asian ghulam (or slaves) and attendants. These have been broadly categorized as Turushkas or Turks" (Verghese 2005: 53). This custom of having Turkish staff in the royal household probably followed the practice of the Delhi sultans, who, from the 13th century onwards, had a considerable number of Turkish ghulams at their service. This was also continued by the Tughlaqs and possibly some of the Turkish slaves and officers, who had come to the Deccan along with the Tughlaq army, eventually arrived at Vijayanagara.

The disintegration of the Tughlaq empire had far-reaching consequences in the political landscape of the Deccan. The vacuum of power subsequent to the Tughlaq supremacy enabled the formation of the Vijayanagara kingdom and the Bahmani sultanate in 1336 and in 1345, respectively. The founders of the Vijayanagara state, Hukka and Bukka, allegedly spent some time at the Tughlaq court in Delhi, first as captives then as officers of Muhammad bin Tughlaq. It is likely that the two brothers were so impressed by the custom of maintaining a large contingent of Turks, that they adopted this practice in their newly formed state. In the second half of the 14th century and during the 15th century both the Vijayanagara and the Bahmani courts offered a wealth of opportunities to many foreigners who poured in not only from the former Tughlaq territories, but also from far afield, such as from Central Asia, Persia, the various Arab lands and Turkey.

TRADERS

The horse trade between Persia, Arabia and Vijayanagara was firmly in the hand of Central Asian and Gulf merchants until well into the 16th century, although, by then, the Portuguese were controlling and licensing the trade (Goetz 1966: 69). As already noted, Central Asian traders, probably Uzbeks, are depicted wearing the traditional attire, the typical pointed caps, occasionally, long pigtails, and riding boots. The evidence of the carvings on the Great Platform (Phase I, south face, west part, fifth row) suggests that they imported not only horses, but also camels, as these animals are also handled by Central Asian grooms.

DANCERS AND MUSICIANS

Among the many depictions of foreigners, dignitaries, merchants, doorkeepers and military personnel carved on the Great Platform, there is one scene which is particularly striking and interesting: a trio of male entertainers in striking costume. The finest depiction of this theme is found on Phase I (south face, west part, 5.2). As already noted, this composition is undoubtedly the clearest of all on the monument, although the third figure which originally completed the group has almost completely disappeared. The right-hand dancer has a pointed beard and conspicuous moustache. He wears a ribbed, pointed cap with upturned brim, and is dressed in a jacket with a 'cloud-collar', a Turkish fashion adopted from the Chinese (Goetz 1966: 69), loose trousers, and holds a long scarf behind his shoulders. The second dancer, who is similarly attired, plays the tambourine. The third dancer, now barely visible, was also depicted striking an animated pose. They all wear pointed slippers. Hanging from their belts are some objects, which although difficult to identify, seem to point to a possible Turkic origin of these performers.[2]

This spirited dancer flanked by a tambourine player – or players – occurs repeatedly at various places on the monument (Phase I, south face, west part, 2.4, 5.2, 5.10, 5.13 and 5.14; west face, south part, 2.2 and north part 2.98; Phase III, East Entrance Chamber, west wall, bottom row, and north wall; lower upana north face 2.5 and east face 2.4). Judging from its frequency, this theme was very popular in the mid to late 14th century, but by the mid 15th century it was slowly going out of fashion. It is interesting to note that this group never appears on sacred monuments.

The question arising at this point is who were these dancers? They were probably courtly entertainers. Interestingly, out of the eleven depictions on the monument seven are concentrated on Phase I. Four are found in row 5, along with the processions of camels, their outlandish grooms and kettledrum-players. Goetz (1966: 69) suggests that these men were Turkish nomads and points out that: 'Their plump, uncouth type recurs in the curious Sino-Turkish nomad figures in the albums of Sultan Muhammad II in the Topkapu Sarai, Stambul. Likewise are their jumping dances, accompanied by a tambourine, characteristic of central Asia.'[3] The fact that they appear together with camels points to their possible Uzbek origin. As already mentioned, Uzbeks were involved in the camel and horse trade. The dancers were soon Indianized. The first hint of this transformation can be seen in Phase IV (middle series, gala, north part, 5). This figure is no longer 'plump, uncouth' but becomes slender and elegant as the tambourine player flanked by two dancing girls. His attire has been modified: the scarf flutters behind his jacket and from the girdle hang three large leaf-shaped elements, slightly reminiscent of the leaf-attire of the tribal hunters. It looks as if this particular costume detail could be derived from the 'cloud-collar' noted in the late 14th-century carving of Phase I, south face. A small, perhaps tiered, cap completes his attire.

The figures of the Turkic dancer and tambourine player coalesced to become the 'folk dancer', one of the most characteristic and ubiquitous figures in Vijayanagara sculpture, found mainly on pillar reliefs in temples. No longer as sturdy as the original figures observed on the Great Platform, and with a conspicuous drooping moustache and pointed beard, the 'folk dancer' carries one or two fly-whisks instead of the long scarf, or plays the tambourine while dancing; the headgear becomes taller, tiered and tapering at the top, somewhat like the crown of a deity. The attire, however, remains similar to that described above. This type of figure was later adopted and further developed in Nayaka sculpture.

FOREIGN RULERS

An exceptional depiction carved on Phase I of the platform shows a foreign ruler, seated cross-legged on a high throne (south face, west part, 4.12). His headgear and what appears to be a long pigtail suggest a Central Asian personage. The stance and attire of the figure recalls that of rulers as depicted in 14th-century Iranian paintings.[4] Unfortunately, on account of the weathered state of the block it is no longer possible to study the details of the costume. At the side of the throne stand two men, their head slightly bent. Both have very distinctive features, dominated by prominent noses. One of the figures has a pointed beard. Both wear long cloaks, whose sleeves cover the hands. This type of cloak, which occurs also in other scenes such as Phase I (south face, west part, 2.9) was fashionable at that time, as demonstrated by Iranian paintings of the late 14th century.[5] Yet another depiction of a foreign ruler, dressed in flowing robes and wearing a tiered headgear, appears in Phase II (south face, 3.26). In this case also, the weathered state of the block makes a precise identification impossible.

DOORKEEPERS

Central Asian doorkeepers appear frequently on the platform: the best examples are those on the rear (west) wall of the East Entrance Chamber of Phase III. Their costumes, carefully rendered by the artists, suggest their belonging to different communities. Three of them wear pointed caps of different shapes, and their hair is gathered in a thick pigtail, and sport pointed beards. The first from left on the bottom row, wears a cloak reaching to the boots, tied to the right, with a belt; the first from the left on the second row, wears an elaborately pleated lower garment, possibly wide riding breeches. Due to the state of the carving it is not clear whether or not he wears boots. The last figure on the second row wears a long cloak with a belt at the waist, and his cap has an elaborate brim, somewhat reminiscent of a crown. The last of the doorkeepers, to the extreme right of the bottom row, seems more at ease that the three just described. He leans nonchalantly on his long staff, wears a turban, and is lightly dressed. Probably, this is a person coming from another part of India, possibly from one of the Deccan states.

NOTES

1. The newcomers' war strategy was far superior to that of the local military. They relied on 'cavalry, Turkish composite bows, armours (sic), guns (a primitive type already in 1366) and a highly developed fortification technique, whereas the Hindus used mainly infantry, armed with spears, swords and shields or long bows, and had only an insufficient cavalry and fortresses of the simplest type, though constructed of very hard stones on sites well protected by nature' (Goetz 1966: 66).
2. Personal communication by George Michell, July 2008.
3. The dance movement and the scarf are similar to those seen in the 15th-century depiction of dancing 'shamans' (Topkapu Saray Museum, Hazine 2153, p. 34 b).
4. Such as 'Humay at the court of the emperor of China', from the *Diwan* of Khwaju Kirmani, 798/1396, British Library Add.18113; fol. 12 a (Gray 1979: 107, fig. 65).
5. Such as 'Malikshah accosted by a poor woman', *Masnavis* of Khwaju Kirmani, 798/1396, British Library, Add. 18113 fol. 85 r. (Sims 2002: 158, fig.7).

GLOSSARY OF INDIAN NAMES AND TERMS

adhishthana, basement consisting of a vertical sequence of mouldings
anjali (mudra), a hand pose of respectful greeting or adoration, in which both hands are clasped together, palms touching
arati, ceremony in which a deity is honoured by waving clockwise around its image a tray containing a lamp
ashvamedha, horse sacrifice; an elaborate ritual performed by kings to extend their power, obtain sons, or atone for a sin
Ashvina, month corresponding to September-October
Bhavani, name of Durga
Chaitra, the first month of the year, corresponding to April-May
chauri, fly whisk
Chenchus, community living in the forests of the Nallaimalai hills in Andhra; claim to be related to Narasimha who married a Chenchu girl.
Chenchu Lakshmi, an aspect of Lakshmi; Chenchu girl with whom Narasimha falls in love
chowkidar, 'doorkeeper'
damaru, hourglass-shaped drum
Dasara, 'tenth day'; the day immediately after the Mahanavami
Devi, goddess, 'great goddess'
Durga, powerful goddess created by the gods to kill Mahishasura
gajavrishabha, decorative motif consisting of a composite half-elephant and half-bull
gala, 'neck', recessed vertical moulding
hamsa, goose
hamsa-mayura, decorative motif combining hamsa and peacock
Indra, lord of the sky, regent of the east
jagati, lower block-like basement moulding
Kaitabha, demon destroyed by Vishnu
kalasha, water-pot, vase, decorative finial in the shape of a water-pot
Kali, goddess of death and destruction, aspect of Devi
Kalyanotsava, annual marriage festival of god and goddess
Kama, Kamadeva, god of love
kantha, recessed vertical moulding in the adhishthana
kapala, skull cup, attribute of various orders of ascetics
kapota, downward curved moulding in a base or above a wall
kirttimukha, 'face of glory'; grimacing lion with floral motifs emanating from its mouth
kolata, folk dance, in which performers carry sticks
kudu, horseshoe-shaped decorative element, projecting out of a kapota
kullayi, cap worn by Vijayanagara nobles
kumbhapanjara, column shaft emerging from a water pot, out of which sprouts foliage; has a panjara shaped capital
kumuda, moulding of adhishthana, placed above jagati and below kapota; may be rounded or three-, seven- or nine-sided (see tripatta-kumuda)
latasundari, maiden clutching a creeper.
lungi, lower male garment wound around the waist
Madhu, demon destroyed by Vishnu
makara, mythical creature, with the body of a crocodile (or dolphin), elephant trunk and foliated tail; symbolises the life-force of the water
Mahabharata, epic poem in 18 books, narrating the adventures of the Pandava princes and

the rivalry with their cousins, the Kauravas.
Mahanavami, nine-day festival, celebrated in September-October; see Navaratri
Mahishasura, buffalo demon killed by Durga
Matsyendranatha, founder of a school of Hindu mysticism
mridanga, large, barrel-shaped drum
Mrigayotsava, annual hunting festival of a temple god
nagabandha, 'snake-band'; decorative element similar to a cobra's head on a pillar shaft
nagasvaram, wind instrument
Narada, divine seer
Narasimha, 'man-lion'; fourth incarnation of Vishnu
Natha, follower of a school of mysticism founded by Gorakhnatha and Matsyendranatha; important centre of the natha tradition was Srisailam
Navaratri 'nine nights' festival, also known as Mahanavami.
padma, lotus; scalloped moulding on adhishthana
Pampa, Pampambika, ancient river goddess, tutelary deity of Hampi
panjara, roof-form with horseshoe-shaped arched projection; capital of a kumbhapanjara
pattika, narrow, projecting adhishthana moulding
pendeya, anklet of honour
purnakumbha, 'vase of plenty'; decorative pot-shaped motif with overflowing foliage
pushpapodikai, pushpapotika, curved bracket ending in a pendant lotus bud
rajasuya, royal consecration
Rati, goddess of lust, consort of Kama
Rama, seventh incarnation of Vishnu; hero of the *Ramayana*
Ramayana, epic work in seven books describing Rama's exploits
Rathotsava, annual chariot festival of a temple
Ravana, mighty king of Lanka, antagonist of Rama in the *Ramayana*
shakha, door jamb
shala, shrine with barrel-vaulted roof
Sita, Rama's wife, abducted by Ravana in the *Ramayana*
torana, arch, doorway
tripatta-kumuda, three-faced kumuda
Tripurasuras, demons of the three cities, eventually destroyed by Shiva
upana, lowest moulding of adhishthana
upapitha, plinth below adhishthana
vajapeya, drink of power
Valmiki, mythical sage, reputed author of the *Ramayana*
Vasanta, spring; the god of spring, often identified with Kama
Vasantotsava, spring-festival
Vijayadashami 'victorious tenth', day following the Mahanavami
vina, string instrument
Virupaksha, 'of misformed eyes'; name of Shiva worshipped in the temple at Hampi
Vritra, giant snake or dragon killed by Indra
yajnopavita, sacred thread
yali, mythical creature, often depicted as a lion with an elephant trunk, generally depicted trampling other animals or human figures
yogapatta, cloth or band tied around the knees and hips

SELECT BIBLIOGRAPHY

Anderson 1993
L.M. Anderson, *Vasantosava, The Spring Festivals of India: Texts & Traditions*, New Delhi: D.K. Printworld.

Balasundram 1941
A.K. Balasundram, *Never to be Forgotten Hampi Ruins in Pictures: Relics of the Glory & Grandeur of the Vijayanagar Empire in Pictures*, Anantapur: Rayalaseema Krishna Raya Publishing Works.

Boner 1993
G. Boner, L. Soni and J. Soni, *Alice Boner Diaries – India 1934-67*, Delhi: Motilal Banarsidass.

Dallapiccola 2001
A.L. Dallapiccola, 'The Great Platform at Vijayanagara', in J.M. Fritz and G. Michell, eds., *New Light on Hampi*, Mumbai: Marg Publications, 63-73.

Dallapiccola 2010
A.L. Dallapiccola, 'Sculptures on the Great Platform at Vijayanagara', in A. Verghese and A.L. Dallapiccola, eds., *South India Under Vijayanagara: Recent Research in Art and Archaeology, 1350-1650*, New Delhi: Oxford University Press.

Dallapiccola and Verghese 1998
A.L. Dallapiccola and A. Verghese, *Sculpture at Vijayanagara: Iconography and Style*, New Delhi: Manohar.

De Warren 1845
E. De Warren, 'Les Ruines de Vijayanagara', *Revue des Deux Mondes*, XI, 148-76.

Devakunjari 1970
D. Devakunjari, *Hampi*, Calcutta: Archaeological Survey of India.

Filliozat 1985
P.-S. Filliozat, 'Technique of chronology and construction in the temple of Vithala at Hampi', in A.L. Dallapiccola and S. Zingel-Ave' Lallemant, eds., *Vijayanagara – City and Empire: New Currents of Research*, Wiesbaden: Franz Steiner Verlag, 1, 296-307.

Filliozat 1999
V. Filliozat, ed., *Vijayanagar as Seen by Domingo Paes and Fernao Nuniz (16th Century Portuguese Chroniclers) and Others*, New Delhi: National Book Trust.

Francis 1904
W. Francis, *Madras District Gazetteer, Bellary*, Madras: The Superintendent, Government Press.

Fritz, Michell and Nagaraja Rao 1984
J.M. Fritz, G. Michell and M.S. Nagaraja Rao, *Where Kings and Gods Meet: The Royal Centre at Vijayanagara, India*, Tucson: University of Arizona Press, and Melbourne: Department of Architecture and Building, University of Melbourne.

Goetz 1966
H. Goetz, 'Muslims in Vijayanagara: The Record of Monuments', in *Studies in Indian Culture: Dr. G. Yazdani Commemoration Volume*, Hyderabad: Maulana Abdul Kalam Azad Oriental Research Institute, 66-70.

Gray 1979
B. Gray, ed., *The Arts of the Book in Central Asia*, London: Serindia.

Kinsley 1996
D. Kinsley, *Hindu Goddesses: Visions of the Divine Feminine in the Hindu Religious Tradition*, Berkeley: University of California Press.

Kotraiah and Dallapiccola 2003
C.T.M. Kotraiah and A.L. Dallapiccola, eds., *King, Court and Capital: An Anthology of Kannada Literary Sources from the Vijaya-*

nagara Period, New Delhi: Manohar.

Krishna Das 1996
A. Krishna Das, 'Preliminary Findings on Divine and Royal Themes in the Chariot Festival at Hampi', in D.V. Devaraj and C.S. Patil, eds., *Vijayanagara, Progress of Research 1988-91*, Mysore: Directorate of Archaeology and Museums, 210-15.

Krishna Das 2006
A. Krishna Das, 'Account of the Chariot Festival at Hampi', in J.M. Fritz, P. Brubaker and T. Raczek, eds., *Vijayanagara. Archaeological Exploration, 1990-2000: Papers in Memory of Channabasappa S. Patil*, New Delhi: Manohar, 1, 319-37.

Longhurst 1925 [1917]
A.H. Longhurst, *Hampi Ruins, Described and Illustrated*, Calcutta: Government of India, Central Publication Branch [Madras: Superintendent Government Press].

Major 1992 [1857]
R.H. Major, *India in the Fifteenth Century: Being a Collection of Narratives of Voyages to India*, New Delhi: Asian Educational Services [London: The Hakluyt Society, XXII].

Meadows Taylor and Fergusson 1866
P. Meadows Taylor and J. Fergusson, *Architecture in Dharwar & Mysore*, London: John Murray.

Michell 1982
G. Michell, 'The Royal Centre and the Great Platform at Vijayanagara', in B. Baumer, ed., *Rupa Pratirupa: Alice Boner Commemoration Volume*, New Delhi: Biblia Impex, 109-18.

Michell 1986
G. Michell, 'Folk Tradition in a Monumental Setting: Sculptures of the Great Platform at Vijayanagara', in L. Chandra and J. Jain, eds., *Dimensions of Indian Art*, Delhi: Agam Kala Prakashan, 287-90.

Michell 1992
G. Michell, 'The Mahanavami Festival at Vijayanagara', *India International Centre Quarterly*, 19/3, 151-61.

Michell and Filliozat 1981
G. Michell and V. Filliozat, eds., *Splendours of the Vijayanagara Empire: Hampi*, Bombay: Marg Publications.

Nagaraja Rao 1988
M.S. Nagaraja Rao, ed., *Vijayanagara through the Eyes of Alexander J. Greenlaw 1856 and John Gollings 1983*, Mysore: Directorate of Archaeology and Museums.

Panchamukhi 1953
R.S. Panchamukhi, *Virupaksha Vasantotsava Champu*, Dharwar: Kannada Research Institute.

Patil and Patil 1995
C.S. Patil and V.C. Patil, *Inscriptions of Karnataka, Volume 1: Inscriptions at Vijayanagara (Hampi)*, Mysore: Directorate of Archaeology and Museums.

Raman 1990
K.V. Raman, 'Architecture of the Vijayanagara Period', in H.M. Nayak and B.R. Gopal, eds., *South Indian Studies*, Madras.

Rangacharya 1919
V. Rangacharya, *Inscriptions of the Madras Presidency*, Madras: Government Press.

Rea 1886-7
A. Rea, 'Vijayanagara', *Christian College Magazine*, December, 428-38, and January, 502-9.

Saletore 1982
R.N. Saletore, *Vijayanagara Art*, Delhi: Sundeep Prakashan.

Sewell 1970 [1900]
R. Sewell, *A Forgotten Empire (Vijayanagara), A Contribution to the History of India*, New Delhi: Asian Educational Services [London: Swan Sonnenschine & Co.].

Sims 2002
E. Sims, *Peerless Images: Persian Painting and its Sources*, New Haven and London: Yale University Press.

Sitapati 1982
P. Sitapati, *Sri Ahobila Narasimha Swamy Temple*, Hyderabad: The Director, Archaeology and Museums, Government of Andhra Pradesh.

Sivapriyananda and Singh Auwa 1995
Sivapriyananda and G. Singh Auwa, *Mysore Royal Dasara*, New Delhi: Abhinav Publications.

Stein 1984
B. Stein, 'Mahanavami: Medieval and Modern Kingly Ritual in South India', in *All the King's Mana: Papers on Medieval*

South Indian History, Madras: New Era Publications, 302-36.

Thackston 1989

W.M. Thackston, ed. and trs., 'Abd Razzaq [Kamaluddin Abdul-Razzaq Samarqandi], Mission to Calicut and Vijayanagar', in *A Century of Princes: Sources on Timurid History and Art*, Cambridge, Mass., The Aga Khan Program for Islamic Architecture, 299-321.

Verghese 1991

A. Verghese, 'Court Attire in Vijayanagara (From a Study of Monuments)', *Quarterly Journal of the Mythic Society*, 82/1, 43-61.

Verghese 1995

A. Verghese, *Religious Traditions at Vijayanagara as Revealed Through the Monuments*, New Delhi: Manohar.

Verghese 2000

A. Verghese, *Archaeology, Art and Religion: New Perspectives on Vijayanagara*, New Delhi: Oxford University Press.

Verghese 2005

A. Verghese, "Cultural Confluence: Influences from Contemporary Sultanates on Vijayanagara Courtly Art and Culture from a Study of the Monuments", *Indo-Koko-Kenkyu – Indian Archaeological Studies*, Vol, 26, Indian Archaeological Society, Tokyo, June 2005, 51-62.

Wagoner 1996

P.B. Wagoner, '"Sultan among Hindu Kings": Dress, Titles and the Islamicization of Hindu Culture at Vijayanagara', *Journal of Asian Studies*, 4, November, 851-80.

Wagoner 2000

P.B. Wagoner, 'Harihara, Bukka and the Sultan: The Delhi Sultanate in the Political Imagination of Vijayanagara', in D. Gilmartin and B.B. Lawrence, eds., *Beyond Turk and Hindu: Shaping Religious Identities in Islamicate India*, Gainesville: University Press of Florida, 300-26.

Wagoner 2007

P.B. Wagoner, 'Retrieving the Chalukyan Past: The Politics of Architectural Reuse in the Sixteenth-Century Deccan', *South Asian Studies*, 23, 1-29.

Wagoner 2010

P.B. Wagoner, 'Retrieving the Chalukyan Past at Sixteenth-Century Vijayanagara: The Stepped Tank in the Royal Centre (IV/6)', in A. Verghese and A.L. Dallapiccola, eds., *South India Under Vijayanagara: Recent Research in Art and Archaeology, 1350-1650*, New Delhi: Oxford University Press.

ABBREVIATIONS

APRASDSC	*Annual Progress Report of the Archaeological Survey Department, Southern Circle*
APRASMC	*Annual Progress Report of the Archaeological Survey of Madras & Coorg*
ARADSC	*Annual Report of the Archaeological Survey, Southern Circle*
ARASI	*Annual Report, Archaeological Survey of India*
ARE	*Annual Report on Epigraphy*
ARIE	*Annual Report on Indian Epigraphy*
SII	*South Indian Inscriptions*

FIGURES AND PLATES

Note: Figures 2 to 6 are folded in a pocket at the back of the volume. Figure 13, see p. 158.

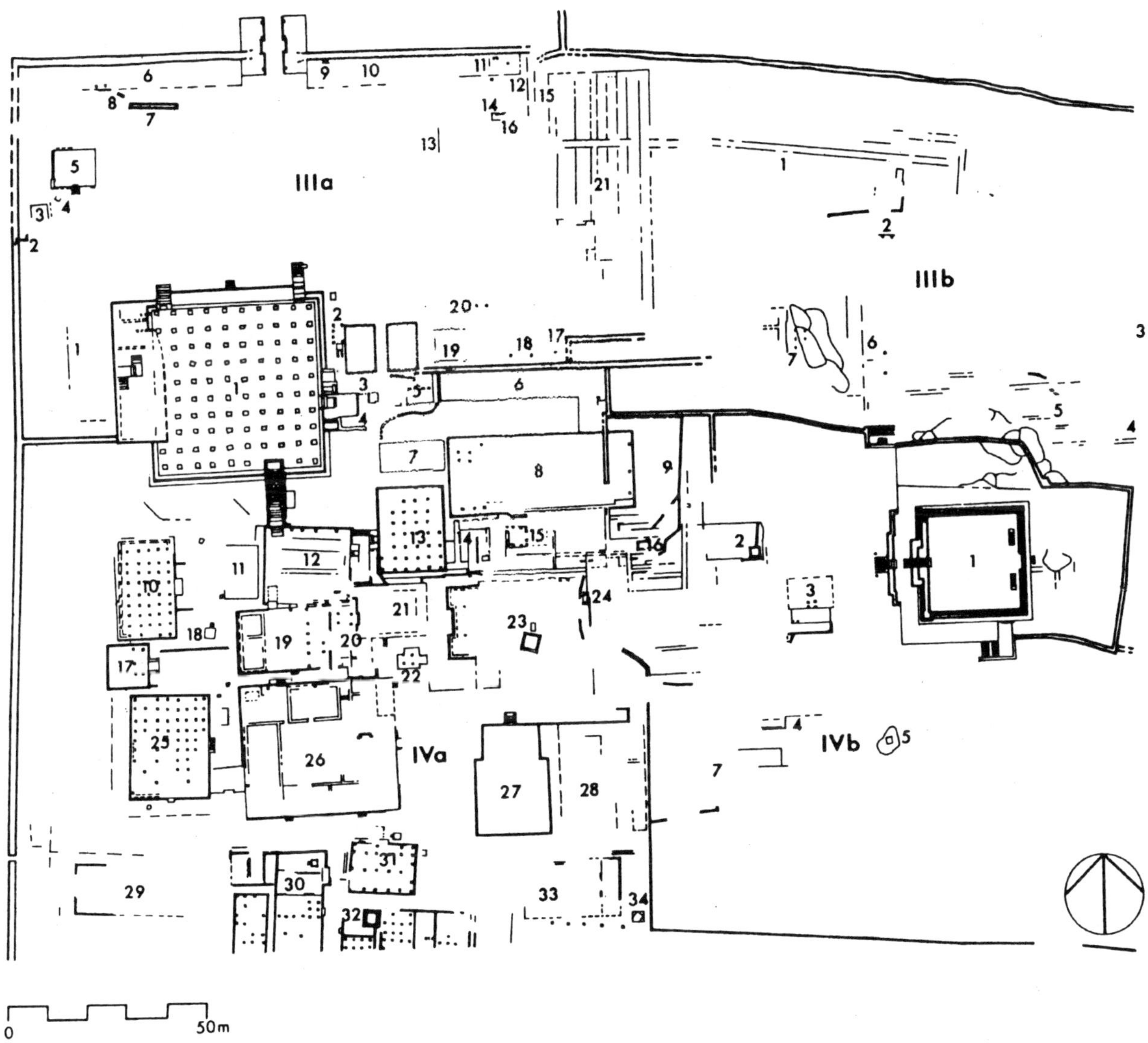

Figure 1: Enclosure IV of the Royal Centre showing the Great Platform in the north-west corner.

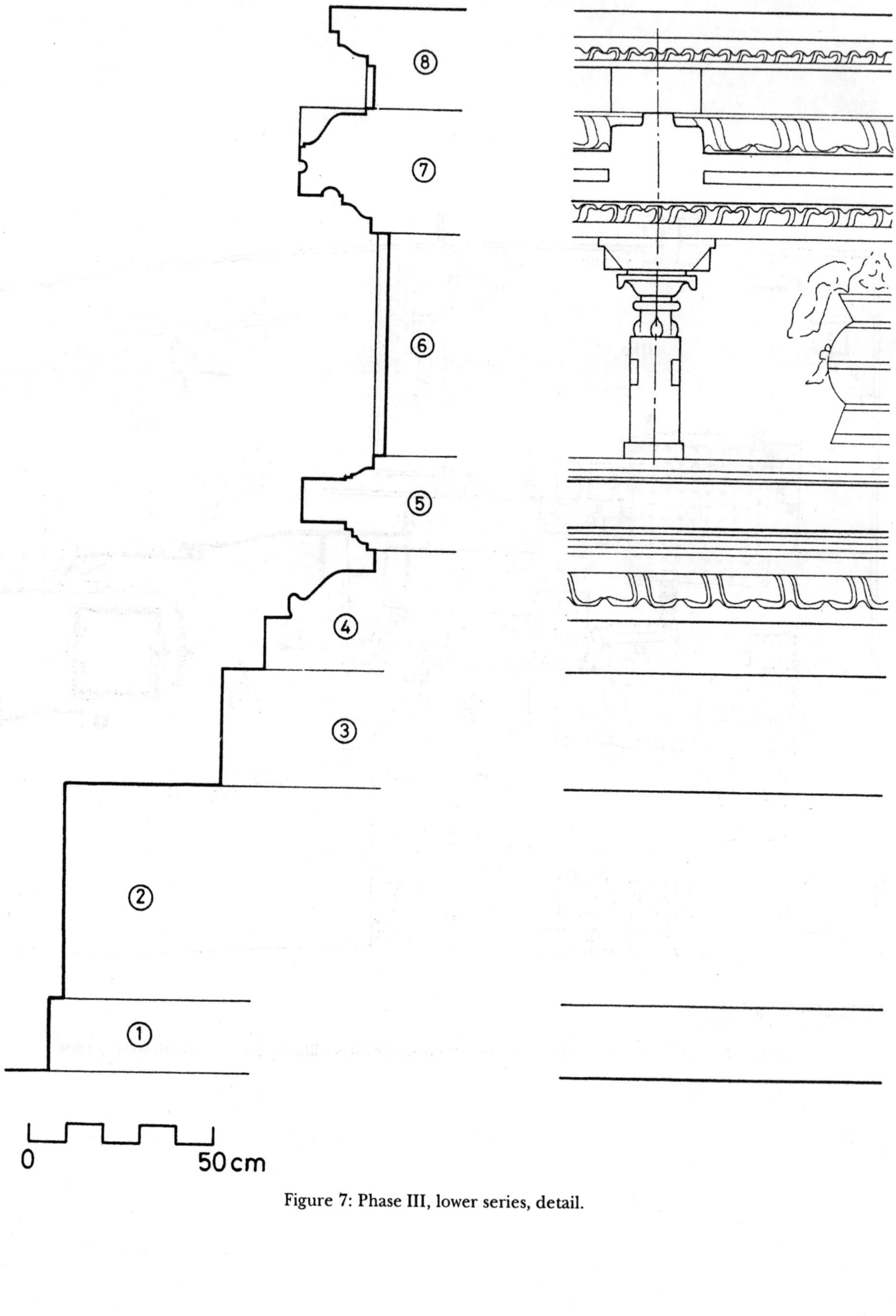

Figure 7: Phase III, lower series, detail.

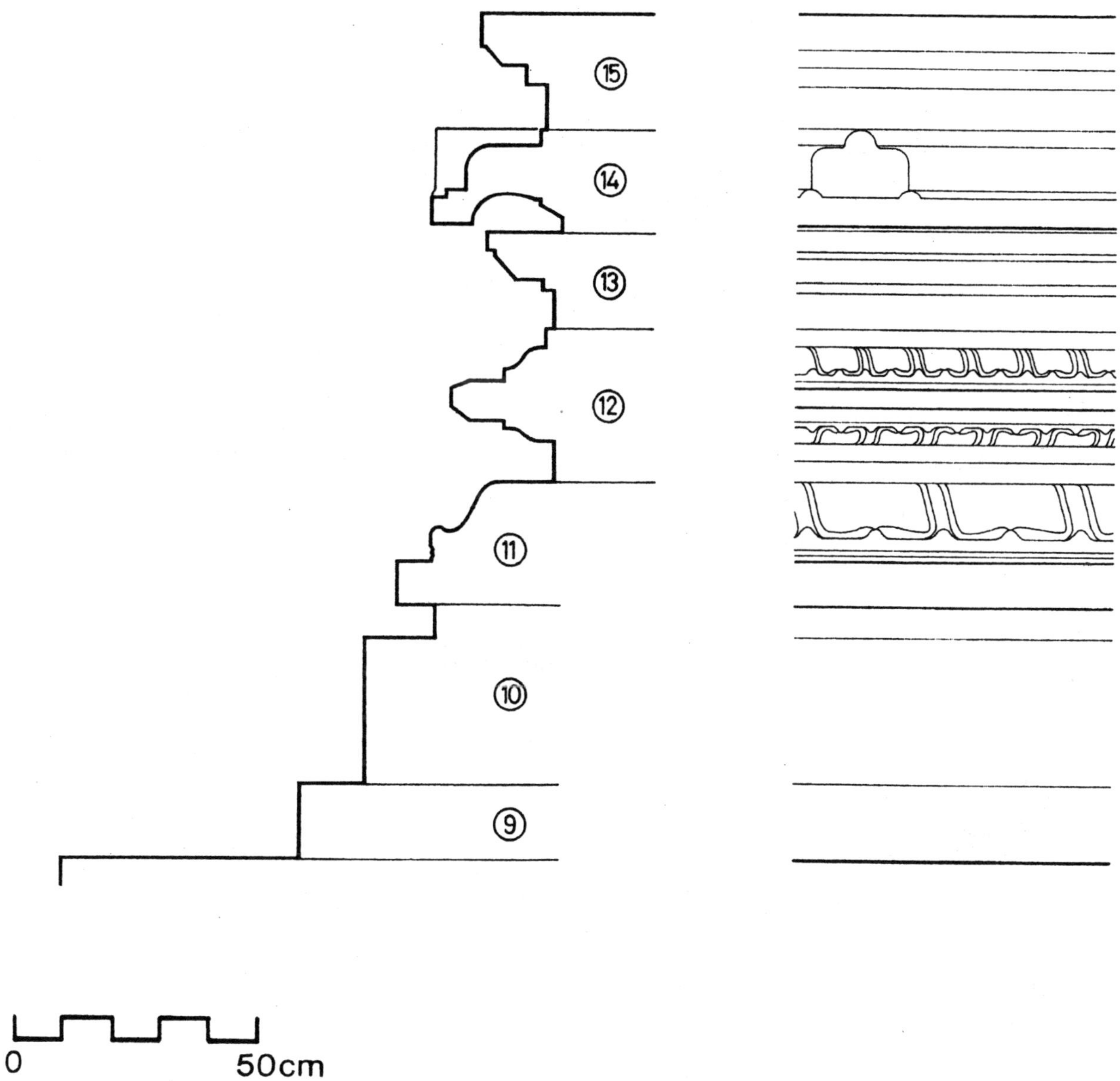

Figure 8: Phase III, upper series, detail.

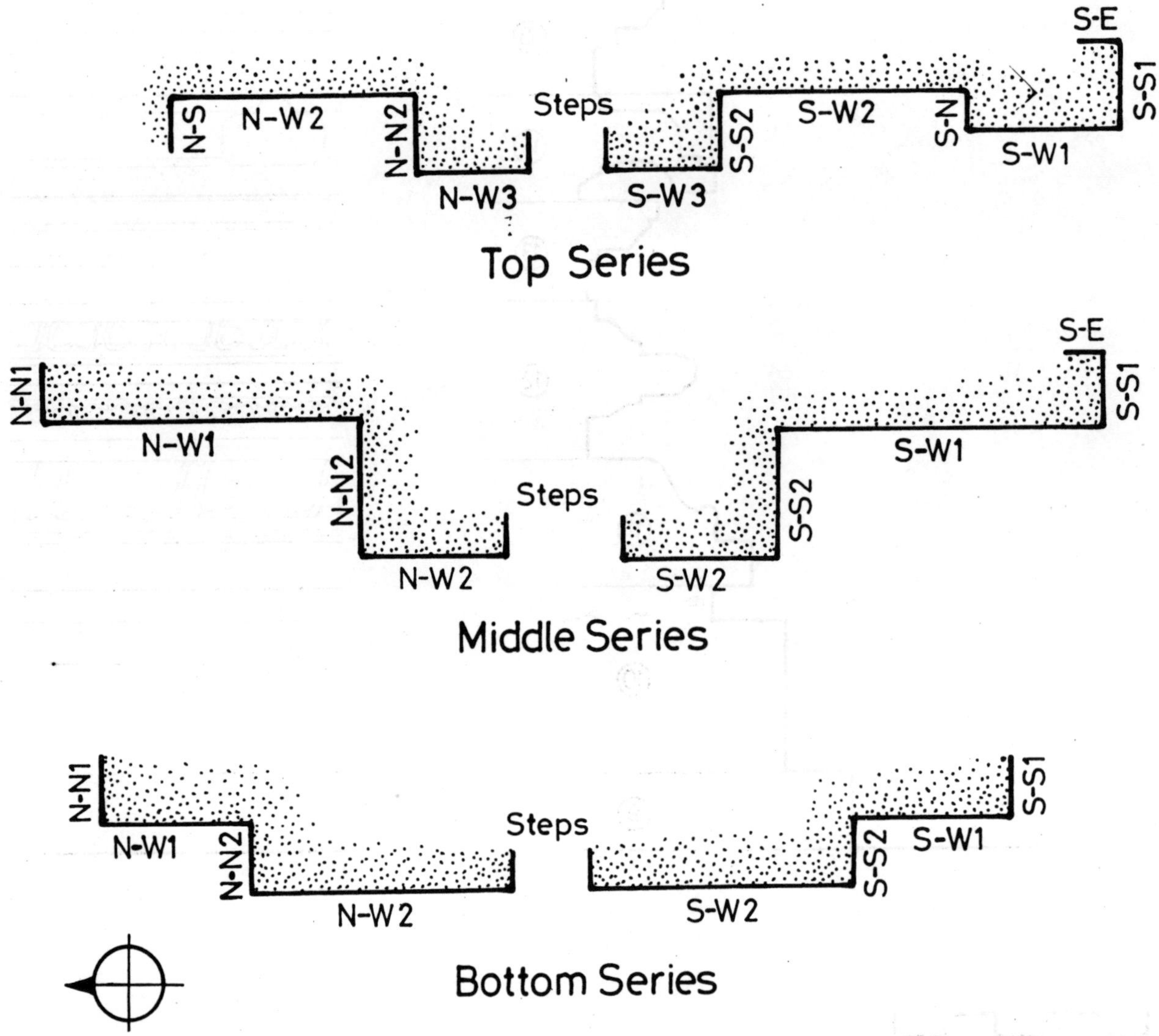

Figure 9: Phase IV, wall segments.

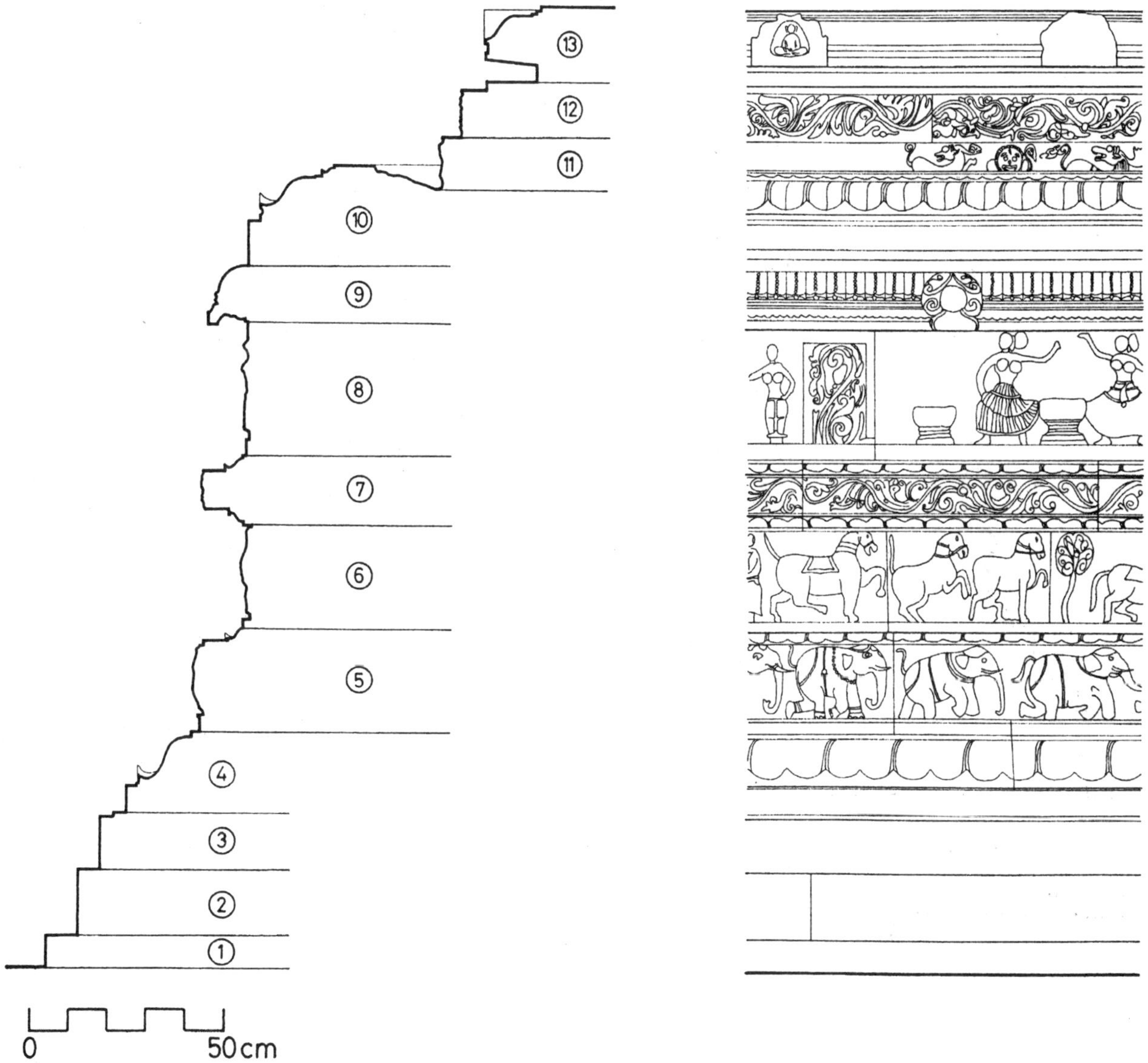

Figure 10: Phase IV, bottom series, detail.

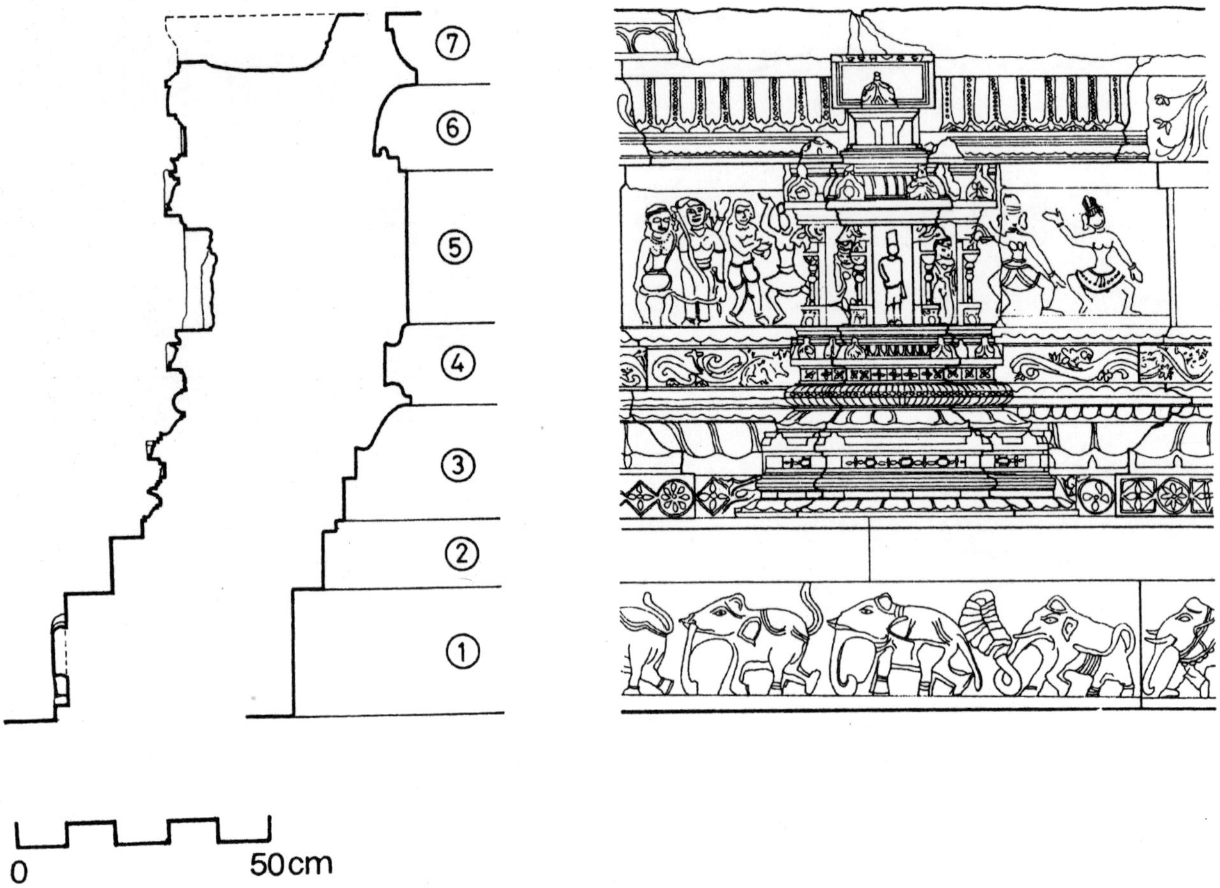

Figure 11: Phae IV, middle series, detail of Niche S1.

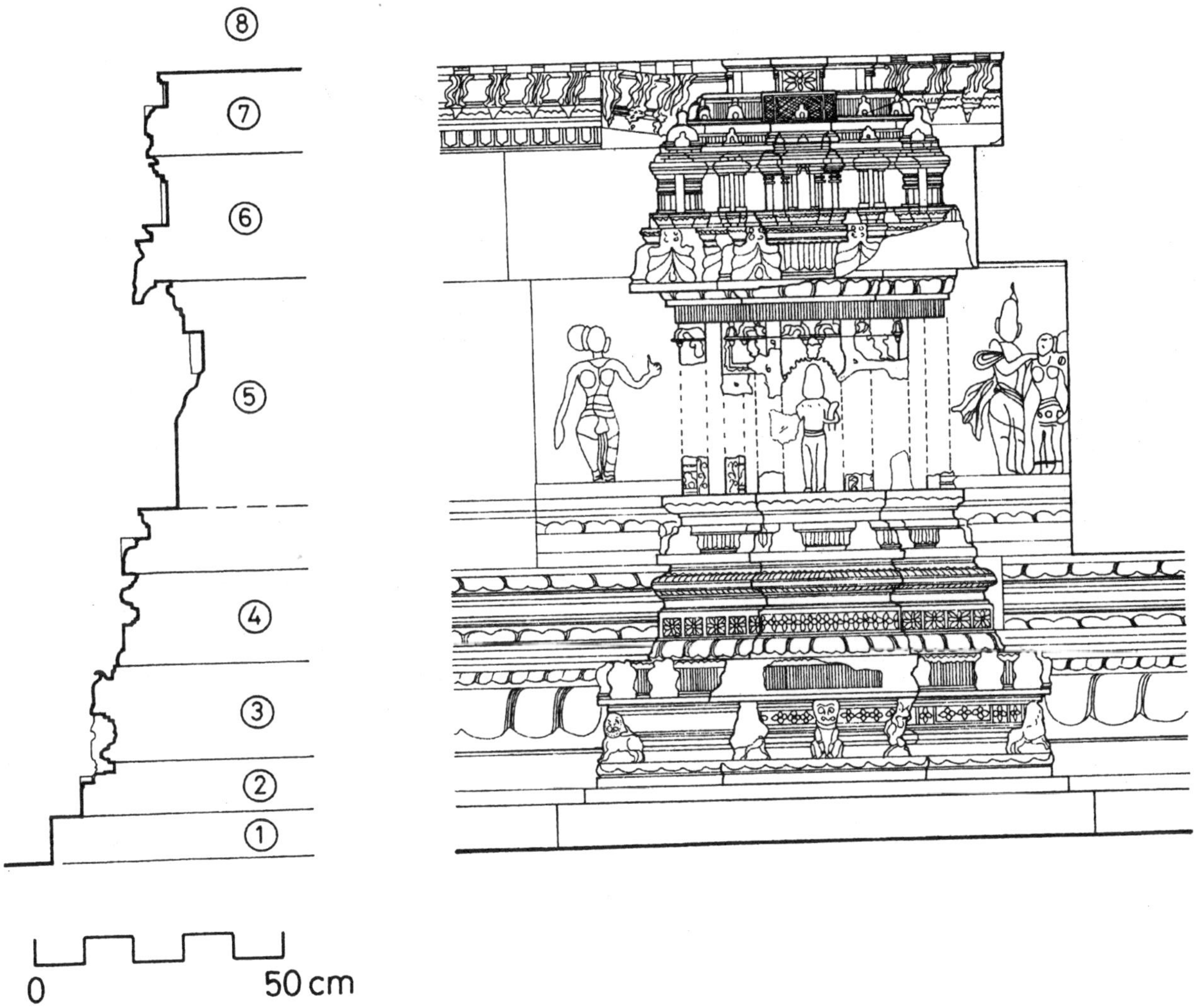

Figure 12: Phase IV, top series, detail of Niche N1.

Plate 1: View from the south-west, before restoration. From Robert Sewell, *A Forgotten Empire (Vijayanagara): A Contribution to the History of India*, London: Swan Sonnenschine & Co., 1900, opposite p. 269.

Plate 2: South face.

Plate 3: South Staircase, south face.

Plate 4: East face.

Plate 5: West face.

Plate 6: Camels, soldier and lady with parrot.
Phase I, south face, east part, blocks 3.12, 3.13 and 4.12.

Plate 7: Hunting scene and camels.
Phase I, south face, east part, blocks 2.5 and 3.12.

Plate 8: Hunting scenes.
Phase I, south face, east part, blocks 2.5 and 2.6.

Plate 9: Hunting scenes, animal parades, musicians and elephants.
Phase I, south face, west part, rows 3 to 6.

Plate 10: Processional frieze.
Phase I, south face, west part, block 2.2.

Plate 11: Parading troops.
Phase I, south face, west part, blocks 2.7 and 2.8.

Plate 12: Soldiers.
Phase I, south face, west part, block 4.3, detail.

Plate 13: Parading troops
Phase I, south face, west part, block 2.7.

Plate 14: Processional friezes, cavalry and camels.
Phase II, south face, west part, blocks 4.10 and 5.12.

Plate 15: Central Asian horseman.
Phase I, west face, south part, block 4.2, detail.

Plate 16: Horsemen and chowkidar.
Phase I, south face, west part, block 4.7.

Plate 17: Horses and grooms
Phase I, south face, west part, block 4.3.

Plate 18: Foreign ruler with traders, and groom leading horse.
Phase I, south face, west part, block 4.12.

Plate 19: Man killing a tiger.
Phase I, south face, west part, block 2.6.

Plate 20: Courtly figure hunting.
Phase I, south face, west part, block 3.1.

Plate 21: Central Asian horseman killing a tiger.
Phase I, west face, south part, block 4.2. detail.

Plate 22: Courtly and tribal hunters.
Phase I, south face, west part, block 3.3.

Plate 23: Hunters and dogs attacking a gazelle.
Phase I, south face, west part, blocks 3.11 and 3.12.

Plate 24: Beater with dogs and hunting scene.
Phase I, south face, west part, blocks 3.6 and 3.7.

Plate 25: Beater and dogs.
Phase I, south face, west part, block 3.6.

Plate 26: Noblemen watching a boxing match.
Phase I, south face, west part, block 2.5.

Plate 27: Boxing match.
Phase I, south face, west part, block 2.5, detail.

Plate 28: Central Asian dancers.
Phase I, south face, west part, block 5.2.

Plate 29: Courtly figure conversing with foreigners.
Phase I, south face, west part, block 2.9.

Plate 30: Royal figure.
Phase I, south face, west part, block 2.9, detail.

Plate 31: Foreign envoys.
Phase I, south face, west part, block 2.9, detail.

Plate 32: Elephant and fabulous beast.
Phase I, south face, west part, block 6.11.

Plate 33: Central Asian chowkidar.
Phase I, west face, south part, block 5.2, detail.

Plate 34: Dancers, musicians and hamsas.
South Staircase, south face, rows 1 to 6.

Plate 35: Narasimha extracting a thorn from Chenchu Lakshmi's foot.
South Staircase, south face, block 1.2.

Plate 36: Hunting scenes.
South Staircase, south face, block 1.3.

Plate 37: Hunting scene.
South Staircase, east face, block 1.1.

Plate 38: Forest scenes and hamsas.
South Staircase, east face, blocks 1.2 and 2.2.

Plate 39: Hamsa.
South Staircase, south face, row 2, detail.

Plate 40: Musicians, stick-dancers and Vasantotsava celebrations.
South Staircase, south face, rows 3, 4 and 5.

Plate 41: Vasantotsava celebrations.
South Staircase, south face, block 5.1 detail.

Plate 42: Stick-dancers and nobleman watching an acrobat.
South Staircase, east face, blocks 3.2 and 4.2.

Plate 43: Elephants and grooms.
South Staircase, south face, block 7.1.

Plate 44: Elephants at work.
South Staircase, east face, block 7.1, detail.

Plate 45: Noblemen and foreign guests and chowkidar.
South Staircase, east face, blocks 7.1 and 7.2.

Plate 46: Yali balustrade.
South Staircase, balustrade, outer (south) face.

Plate 47: Visual pun.
South Staircase, balustrade, outer (south) face.

Plate 48: Central Asian chowkidar.
South Staircase, balustrade, inner (north) face.

Plate 49: Yali and Central Asian chowkidar.
South Staircase, balustrade, inner (north) face.

Plate 50: Monkey and tree.
South Staircase, reused slab on steps.

Plate 51: Elephants with riders.
Phase II, south face, sculpted boulder, 2A and 2B.

Plate 52: Horse traders, courtly figure, elephants and hamsas.
Phase II, south face, blocks 4.1, 5.1 to 5.4 and 6.1.

Plate 53: Traders with courtly figures.
Phase II, south face, blocks 3.25 to 3.27.

Plate 54: Wrestlers.
Phase II, south face, block 3.22.

Plate 55: State horse.
Phase II, south face, block 4.38.

Plate 56: Hunter attacked by tigers.
Phase II, south face, blocks 3.7, 3.8 and 4.15.

Plate 57: Hunting scenes.
Phase II, east face, south part, block 4.92.

Plate 58: Gazelle and lady with parrot flanked by chowkidars.
Phase II, south face, blocks 3.35 and 3.36.

Plate 59: Tiger riding on an elephant and leaping gazelle.
Phase II, south face, blocks 3.34 and 3.35.

Plate 60: Natha riding a lion and monkeys beside tree.
Phase II, south face, blocks 3.29 and 4.39.

Plate 61: General view.
Phase II, west face, north part, rows 5 and 6.

Plate 62: Enraged elephants with attendants.
Phase II, west face, north part, block 6.97.

Plate 63: Elephants and frieze of hamsas and lotuses.
Phase III, south face, east part.

Plate 64: Wrestlers and elephant.
Phase III, north face, block 2.1.

Plate 65: Central Asian dancer and elephants.
Phase III, east face, block 2.4.

Plate 66: Dancing scene and elephant with groom.
Phase III, east face, block 2.6.

Plate 67: Central Asian dancer and musicians.
East Entrance Chamber, north wall.

Plate 68: Central Asian horse-trader and chowkidar.
East Entrance Chamber, south wall.

Plate 69: Central Asian chowkidars, musicians and animal attendants.
East Entrance Chamber, rear (west) wall.

Plates 70 and 71: Central Asian dancer and chowkidar.
East Entrance Chamber, rear (west) wall, first and second rows.

Plates 72 and 73: Central Asian man with bird, and chowkidar.
East Entrance Chamber, rear (west) wall, second row.

Plate 74: Purnaghata.
Phase III, south face, lower gala, 4.

Plate 75: Architectural portal.
Phase III, south face, lower gala, 4.

Plate 76: Medallion with knotted design.
Phase III, south face, lower gala, 4.

Plate 77: Architectural portal.
Phase III, south face, lower gala, 5.

Plate 78: Medallion with 12 petals.
Phase III, south face, lower gala, 5.

Plate 79: Lotus within square medallion and hamsa.
Phase III, south face, lower gala, 1.

Plate 80: Tiger hunt.
Phase IV, bottom series, course 6, north part, 6.

Plate 81: Fragment of a battle scene.
Phase IV, bottom series, course 6, south part, 17 and 18.

Plate 82: Courtly couple and female attendants.
Phase IV, bottom series, courses 8 and 9, north part, 9.

Plate 83: Female dancers.
Phase IV, bottom series, course 8, north part, 16.

Plate 84: Enraged elephant with attendants.
Phase IV, middle series, course 1, north part, 11.

Plate 85: Enraged elephant with attendants.
Phase IV, middle series, course 1, south part, 15.

Plate 86: Scenes of music and dance.
Phase IV, middle series, course 5, north part, Niche N1.

Plate 87: Dancers and choreographer.
Phase IV, middle series, course 5, north part, 5.

Plate 88: Central Asian musician and female dancers.
Phase IV, middle series, course 5, north part, 5.

Plate 89: Courtly figure with three visitors.
Phase IV, middle series, course 5, south part, 12.

Plate 90: Courtly figure with female attendants receiving visitors.
Phase IV, middle series, course 5, south part, 9.

Plate 91: Niches S1 and S2.
Phase IV, middle and top series, south part.

Plate 92: Courtly figures, kumbhapanjara and Niche N1.
Phase IV, top series, courses 5 and 6, north part.

Plate 93: Couple embracing.
Phase IV, top series, courses 5 and 6, north part.

Plate 94: Chowkidar, kumbhapanjara and maiden.
Phase IV, top series, courses 5 and 6, north part.

Figure 13: Vasantotsava celebrations
Phase IV, missing block.
Line drawing after A.H. Longhurst, *Hampi Ruins, Described and Illustrated*, Calcutta: Government of India, 1917, p. 65.